Senators Beholden
to the People

ALSO BY RICHARD LAWRENCE MILLER
AND FROM MCFARLAND

Money in American Politics: The First 200 Years (2021)

*Lincoln and His World: Volume 4,
The Path to the Presidency, 1854–1860* (2012)

*Lincoln and His World: Volume 3, The Rise to
National Prominence, 1843–1853* (2011)

Senators Beholden to the People
Lincoln and the Doctrine of Instruction

RICHARD LAWRENCE MILLER

McFarland & Company, Inc., Publishers
Jefferson, North Carolina

ISBN (print) 978-1-4766-9171-8
ISBN (ebook) 978-1-4766-5090-6

Library of Congress and British Library
cataloguing data are available

Library of Congress Control Number 2023051296

© 2024 Richard Lawrence Miller. All rights reserved

No part of this book may be reproduced or transmitted in any form or by any means, electronic or mechanical, including photocopying or recording, or by any information storage and retrieval system, without permission in writing from the publisher.

On the cover: President Abraham Lincoln, portrait, seated and facing front, Brady's National Photographic Portrait Galleries, January 8, 1864, printed later, 1909 (Library of Congress); *background* Senate Chamber, in U.S. Capitol, Bell & Bro. (Washington, D.C.), between 1860 and 1930 (Library of Congress)

Printed in the United States of America

*McFarland & Company, Inc., Publishers
Box 611, Jefferson, North Carolina 28640
www.mcfarlandpub.com*

To James Cornelius, Roy Fox,
Pat Schneider, and Nancy Clark

Forms of a constitution may long remain, after its spirit has been entirely extinguished.
—James Brugh, *Political Disquisitions: Or, an Inquiry into Public Errors,* 1774

Table of Contents

Preface   1

Part 1. Instruction   5
Part 2. Election of Senators by State Legislatures   43
Part 3. Lincoln's Experiences with U.S. Senate Campaigns   91

Epilogue: A Modest Proposal   109
Chapter Notes   111
Bibliography   117
Index   121

Preface

I invested twenty years of my life in producing a four-volume exploration of Abraham Lincoln's pre-presidential years. Voluminous as that treatment is, too many aspects of Lincoln's career still had to be omitted. The present book examines an important topic that my Lincoln biography didn't have room to treat. That topic is the doctrine of instruction. I had never heard of the doctrine and found it ever more fascinating as my research developed. A doctrine allowing ordinary citizens to call a public meeting to expel members of Congress and other government officials is an idea with much appeal at the beginning of the twenty-first century. Moreover, knowing about the doctrine puts an unaccustomed meaning on some political rhetoric of Lincoln's era.

In Lincoln's time two types of democracy existed in the United States. There was the "representative democracy" chosen by authors of the federal Constitution and familiar to students of any civics class in high school or college. But at the time the Constitution was adopted a competing form of democracy called "direct democracy" was popular. In representative democracy voters selected members of Congress and other officials to make governmental decisions on their behalf. In direct democracy voters gathered in meetings to ascertain feelings on one issue or another and to then pass resolutions expressing the public will, as in the classic New England town meeting.

"Instruction" was an important element of direct democracy. A meeting's resolution was more than a petition. It was an order from the public that government officials had to obey. If, in good conscience they could not obey, they were expected to resign. Loss of office was an extra-legal penalty having little sanction in law. Support for direct

Preface

democracy was so strong, however, that officeholders disobeyed at their peril. As we shall see, members of Congress, including U.S. Senators, actually departed Congress when a voter meeting forwarded instructions that the officials refused to obey.

In Lincoln's pre-presidential career about 20 percent of Illinois residents could cast ballots. Nonetheless, despite limits on suffrage, direct democracy, combined with the doctrine of instruction, gave nineteenth-century voters far more influence than is possessed by twenty-first-century voters.

In the nineteenth century U.S. Senators were chosen by state legislatures, not by popular election. Agitation arose for changing the Constitution to make Senators electable by the people rather than by their representatives in the state legislature. Although this movement post-dated Lincoln's life, he was affected by the problems that proponents of popular suffrage sought to address. We shall use Lincoln as a case study of how direct democracy affected campaigns for the U.S. Senate.

Although Lincoln's admirers largely view him as the personification of American ideals, some of his ideals were expressed in ways unfamiliar to people today. Lincoln would perhaps be puzzled about what the federal government became. Today his manner of governing might even be rejected by courts and the American people. *Senators Beholden to the People: Lincoln and the Doctrine of Instruction* explores the way democratic government operated in Lincoln's world and how politicians and officials implemented what they believed democracy to be. As we shall see, two kinds of democracy competed for dominance in Lincoln's time, direct democracy (involving the doctrine of instruction under which citizens had the right to command elected officials) and representative democracy (in which elected officials made decisions on behalf of citizens). Each had its proponents and opponents.

This book opens by examining colonial and early republic days, expands into the nineteenth and twentieth centuries, and examines how Lincoln and his associates dealt with laws and customs governing their conduct.

Preface

Let us begin traveling through a world superficially familiar but whose heart was as alien as any found in science fiction.

Political parties occasionally change their names. Tracking those changes is irrelevant to the subject of this book, so I use the term "Whig" in referring to all politicians who opposed Andrew Jackson and "Democrat" for his supporters (who sometimes called themselves "Republican"). Spelling and capitalization of quoted material is modernized in most instances. To reduce confusion, lowercase uses of the word "territory" refer to a geographical expanse and uppercase uses of "Territory" refer to a governmental division. Lowercase capitalization of titles such as "representative," "senator," and "governor" signify a state or Territorial official. Uppercase signifies a federal or colonial official.

PART 1

Instruction

Mastering something called "the doctrine of instruction" was one of the most important skills that successful politicians in Lincoln's era had to learn. Sometimes called the right of instruction, the doctrine is almost forgotten today. But in its time the doctrine was hotly debated. This dispute may be unapparent to modern readers who examine documents from the time, readers who are unfamiliar with terminology signifying discussion of the issue. Components of the doctrine interlocked like pieces of a jigsaw puzzle, bewildering at first but making perfect sense to Lincoln and his colleagues who understood the big picture.

"Instruction" meant that the constituency that elected an official had a right to assemble during his term of office and instruct him to take a particular stance on a controversy. If the officeholder felt unable to obey he was supposed to resign. Honesty and morality were not factors; the official was being forced out of office because of his stance on some public issue. None of this was codified in the U.S. Constitution. Some support for the custom is found in state constitutions and statutes but still it was mostly tradition. Size mattered with the meetings. A U.S. Senator might feel compelled to obey a gathering of temperance activists or slavery opponents drawn from an entire congressional district, open to everyone, and which was called by notices in newspapers. A Senator might not feel so impressed by a resolution of instruction from an unpublicized meeting in the upper floor of a tavern, a gathering comprised of idlers and travelers passing through. Common sense governed expectations of how an elected official would respond. A big, well-organized meeting could compel an official to resign. This actually happened, as we shall see. Here is a typical notice, from colonial times, for a meeting to discuss the Stamp Act.¹

> The Freeholders and other inhabitants of the Town of Braintree qualified to vote in town affairs, being assembled at the Meeting House in the middle precinct of said town pursuant to warrants for assembling said town to inform their Representative expecting their sentiments relative to the Stamp Act and other matters of grievance. Also to see if the town will instruct their Representative on this important and alarming occasion, assembled as aforesaid, Mr. Norton Quincy, Moderator.

At that meeting future President John Adams was a key opponent of the Stamp Act. He later wrote, "This Year 1765 was the epoch of the Stamp Act.... I drew up a petition to the Select Men of Braintree, and procured it to be signed by a number of the respectable inhabitants, to call a meeting of the town to instruct their Representatives in relation to the stamps. The public attention of the whole continent was alarmed, and my principle and political connections were well known.... I prepared a draught of instructions, at home." Referring to that occasion the *Massachusetts Gazette* reported: "We hear from Braintree that the freeholders and other inhabitants of that town, legally assembled on Tuesday the twenty fourth of September last, unanimously voted, that instructions should be given their representative, for his conduct in General Assembly."² Such meetings were common. Here is a report of another, this one from 1774: "The town met yesterday for the choice of members to represent them in the general court to be held next month at Salem. The old members were elected. The town today voted to instruct them."³

Upon adoption of the U.S. Constitution the doctrine of instruction was mainly found as ammunition in a congressional dispute. Most Senators who were faced with instruction were being faced by instruction from their state legislature. U.S. Senators paid attention to citizen desires but were elected by the state legislature and thereby had a constituency of maybe 100 persons. A state legislature that elected the Senators had no hesitation about instructing them to take a particular stance on an issue.

Some U.S. Senators fudged, saying they supported the concept of

Part 1. Instruction

instruction but that resolutions they received from their state legislature had some technicality that invalidated them. Senators John Niles (D–CT) and Perry Smith (D–CT) argued more subtly against the doctrine of instruction. They granted that U.S. Senators were elected by state legislatures but argued that state legislators were not the true constituents, that instead the entire populace of a state was a U.S. Senator's constituency. This was an advanced attitude, little heard of while the doctrine of instruction reigned, but it was eventually adopted via the seventeenth amendment to the Constitution. The two skeptical Senators, Niles and Smith, maintained, "The right of instruction exists, if at all, not in the [state] General Assembly, but in the people, and could be exercised by you [state legislators] for their benefit only."[4] The stance of these two U.S. Senators was unusual for the era.

Tax collectors were objects of public wrath (Library of Congress).

The *Pennsylvania Journal* ran this satirical advertisement on October 24, 1765, to protest passage of the Stamp Act. The skull and crossbones symbolized death of the free press resulting from the passage of the Act (Library of Congress).

Public meetings might instruct Senators, but usually such gatherings targeted U.S. Representatives. Representatives received slightly more polite handling, being "requested" instead of "instructed" to assume a stance, treatment less abrupt probably because they were elected by thousands of voters in a congressional district instead of by a few dozen state legislators, giving the Representatives more prestige in some circles than Senators enjoyed. Although response to such "requests" may have been voluntary, Representatives understood that obedience was expected. Tennessee's U.S. Rep. John Crockett (son of Davy) exploded when the Tennessee legislature "requested" him to support one of President Jackson's banking policies. Crockett "spoke with some warmth" and "denied the right of the present legislature

Part 1. Instruction

to instruct him, for reasons which he gave at length."[5] This expectation of obedience from congressional constituents irked Democrat U.S. Rep. Francis Pickens (a gentleman perhaps best remembered as governor of South Carolina when it bombarded Fort Sumter), who protested "against the instructions emanating from cross-road meetings, and log cabin and tavern gatherings. Were they [U.S. Representatives] to be influenced by the dictates of men who knew nothing of the subjects of which they spoke?" Pickens admonished colleagues, "Do not come here as the miserable tools of party, or of popular assemblages."[6] As Pickens owned 276 slaves, his complaint about instruction may have related more to his wealthy aristocratic background than to philosophical differences about representative democracy versus direct democracy.

Pickens did not speak for everyone. The issue of instruction provided grist for political philosophers overseas as well. From London, England, James Brugh wrote, "It would be an honor to receive instructions and to be responsible to them, would not be beneath the dignity of any person whatever."[7]

For our purposes, in this book I have mostly limited examples to instructions and requests found in the *Congressional Globe*. As noted by the great student of this topic, Peverill

Davy Crockett's son John was not only a tavern keeper in Morristown, Tennessee, but a member of Congress who was offended by instructions from his state legislature (Wikimedia Commons).

Senators Beholden to the People

Squire,[8] *Congressional Globe* provides us plenty to work with. Instructions could come from many sources.

Famed statesmen bickered about the doctrine, and their conclusions sometimes dictated congressional votes on legislation. This was no small thing. In addition to congressional election decisions, other state legislature decisions (say, on banking or railroads) could be governed by the instruction doctrine, with local voters instructing state legislators. During the decades of its use, instruction had daily impact on American life. That import grew as people realized the doctrine raised more questions than it answered. Perhaps the most important question was whether the general population of voters or their representatives speaking on the public's behalf should decide public policy controversies. Pushed to an extreme, the doctrine of instruction would invalidate the U.S. Constitution, allowing Representatives to be recalled after one year in office (see New Jersey Bill of Rights of 1789): "The people reserve unto themselves the power to recall, after at least one

Expectation of obedience from congressional constituents irked Democrat U.S. Rep. Francis Pickens, who protested "against the instructions emanating from cross-road meetings, and log cabin and tavern gatherings." Pickens admonished colleagues, "Do not come here as the miserable tools of party, or of popular assemblages." As he was the owner of 276 slaves, his complaint about instruction may have related more to his wealthy aristocratic background than to philosophical differences about representative democracy versus direct democracy (Charleston Museum via Wikimedia Commons).

Part 1. Instruction

year of service, any elected official in this State or representing this State in the United States Congress. (The Legislature shall enact laws to provide for such recall elections.)" Under the doctrine Senators could be recalled from office despite being elected to a six-year term, and presidents could be recalled by the Electoral College despite having a four-year term, and ordinary voters could be permitted to decide government policy through a town meeting style of direct democracy.

Indeed the doctrine's significance was discussed by the Founding Fathers, who were familiar with political thought extending beyond classic Enlightenment figures. For instance, John Adams was in contact with James Brugh,[9] a British thinker active in the 1770s. In 1774 Adams thanked Brugh for writing *Political Disquisitions*:

> I cannot but think those Disquisitions, the best Service, that a Citizen, could render to his Country, at this great and dangerous Crisis, when the British Empire Seems ripe for Destruction, and tottering on the Brink of a Precipice. If any Thing can possibly open the Eyes of the Nation and excite it to exert itself, it must be such a sight of its Danger, and of the imperceptible Steps, by which it ascended to it.
>
> I have contributed Somewhat to make the Disquisitions more known and attended to in several Parts of America, and they are held in as high Estimation by all my Friends as they are by me, and the more they are read the more eagerly and generally they are sought for.

Brugh saw instruction as crucial to the election process. Said he, "If the members of the house of commons are not obliged to regard the instructions of their constituents; the people of this country chuse a set of despots..., and are as perfect slaves as the Turks, excepting the few months of a general election."[10]

In 1755 Benjamin Franklin noted another way that constituents in the province could enforce their will: "Should our Constituents, when they chose us to represent them in Assembly, not only *instruct* us, but even take Bonds of us."[11] Thus, in colonial Pennsylvania, if someone violated instructions, the penalty could be more than loss of office; the loss could involve a cash amount. In colonial Pennsylvania even British officials weren't immune to instructions by citizens. In 1758 Richard Jackson told Franklin, "It seems reasonable to me, that the Proprietary's

Lieutenant Governor [Pennsylvania's] should reside there, tho,' not uninstructed quite, yet free from any unreasonable Restraint, so that ... he should be *instructed* to pass some Laws, and to refuse others."[12] In 1759 a Privy Council order responding to a petition from Franklin said that commissioners coming to a meeting should "come properly *instructed*, and prepared, to support the Claims of their Constituents."[13] Note that British colonial officials recognized that colonial business in London might be impossible to conduct without instructions from the New World. In subsequent colonial times Thomas Paine spoke of the Pennsylvania general assembly being controlled by instructions.

Foreign Doctrines

Other countries' experience with instruction is scanty; freedom of speech was unheard of in most places. For this topic we would experience little profit from perusal of acts promulgated by European monarchs. There are nonetheless examples of autocrats being faced down by members of popular assemblies who were speaking the desires of their constituents. James Madison was not the only writer who noted that in Switzerland, a federation of several cantons, laws did not take effect unless the populace voted its approval via direct democracy; voters also retained the right of instruction. Likewise, upon instructions from constituents, members of British parliaments thwarted desires of British monarchs, as also happened with those in Spain, France, Ireland, and the German states.

In Britain some persons viewed the Magna Carta of the year 1215 as making instruction a live issue, with barons sending representatives to parliament rather than personally attending, the representatives having to obey the barons rather than vote as they wished. In the mid–1300s an answer to the king's request for supplies was delayed until the commons ascertained their constituents' desire. In the 1830s the journal *Southern Literary Messenger* published an article containing valuable references to other British examples. (The *Messenger* was a distinguished publication of its time; staff members included Edgar Allan Poe. As, however, the *Chicago Manual of Style* was not

Part 1. Instruction

au courant in that era, the *Messenger* article's citations are sometimes difficult to track.) Quoting sources such as William Petyt's *Ancient Right of the Commons* and Gordon's *History of Parliament*, the *Messenger* observes "if any new project was proposed in Parliament for raising subsidies or supplies, the Commons usually replied thereto that they were not *instructed* by their principals in that matter, or that they durst not consent to such tax without conference with the counties." The *Messenger* article cited Blackstone's writings as supporting instruction, that House of Commons members had to vote in the way demanded by their constituents, although an opposite attitude toward instruction, in Blackstone, is indicated by British writer James Brugh in a multi-volume study titled *Political Disquisitions*, published in 1774. Brugh argued, "It is notorious, that the right of constituents to instruct their [parliamentary] members, and the consequent duty of members to obey instructions, is in our times questioned by many, and by many given up. Yet it is certain ... that no harm could come from the members of parliament being obliged to wait for instructions from their constituents."[14] He also noted a side issue, that some

> argue, that members of parliament are not obliged to obey instructions of their constituents, because the constituents do not hear the [parliamentary] debates, and therefore cannot be supposed judges of the matter to be voted.... The very truth is, that the members [of parliament] have no opportunity of being at all better judges of most matters to be voted in parliament than men of understanding and reading, who never sat in the house. So that the hearing of the debates gives no such mighty advantage to the members above the constituents.[15]

Brugh quotes the following message from a group of constituents who no doubt helped the parliament member understand what was expected of him: "We the citizens of London who have cheerfully elected you to serve us in parliament, and thereby committed to your trust the safety, liberty, property, and privileges of ourselves and posterity, think it our duty, as it is our undoubted right, to acquaint you with what we desire and expect from you in discharge of the great trust we repose in you, and what we take to be your duty as our representative."[16]

Senators Beholden to the People

Power to the People

The doctrine of instruction gave a tremendous base of power to American voters. Fisher Ames, who was a federalist, addressed the Massachusetts convention called to ratify the U.S. Constitution: "While the Senators are seated for six years they are admonished of their *responsibility to the state legislatures.*"[17] At the same Massachusetts meeting another speaker (Mr. King) added, "The Senators will have a powerful check, in those men who wish for their seats, who will *watch* their whole conduct in the general government and will *give the alarm* in case of misbehavior." Said King, "The state *legislatures,* if they find their *delegates* erring, and will *instruct them....* When they hear the voice of the people *solemnly dictating* to them *their duty,* they will be bold men indeed to act *contrary to it.*" "These will not be instructions sent them in a private letter which can be put in their pockets; they will be public instructions, which all the country will see; and they will be hardy men indeed to violate them."[18] Less hearty men informed instructors and news editors that they consented to the instruction and then behind the scenes worked to defeat the measure. Pennsylvania's Senator (and future U.S. President) James Buchanan (D–PA) played that trick in 1838 and again in 1842, pledging to obey instructions from the state general assembly while using his influence to thwart the legislature.[19]

When James Buchanan was a U.S Senator from Pennsylvania he pledged to obey instructions but used trickery to evade his promises (Library of Congress).

Part 1. Instruction

Senator Robert Strange (D–NC) declared, "I accepted the trust I now hold, under the full knowledge that those who sent me here expected me to obey instructions when received, or resign. Such is the creed of the political party that elected me."[20] Elected officials were expected to obey instructions from constituents, whether they be on foreign affairs, banking, or railroads. Disobedience carried a stigma that could haunt an official who ran for reelection. As we shall see, some U.S. Senators resigned rather than face voter wrath, especially if they opposed the instructions they received. Regarding officeholders, political thinkers noted that "whensoever any of them has the misfortune not to satisfy the major part of *those that chose him*, he is sure to be rejected *with disgrace* the next time he shall desire to be chosen."[21]

Robert Strange of North Carolina served in the U.S. Senate during the 1830s, where he was an ally of President Andrew Jackson. He was elected to the Senate as a replacement for the Whig Willie Magnum, who resigned rather than obey instructions that he opposed.

Strange ran into his own trouble with instructions when the North Carolina legislature became dominated by Jackson opponents who disagreed with Strange's vote favoring Senator Thomas Hart Benton's resolution expunging criticism of Jackson from the U.S. Senate *Journal*. Strange's stance resulted in his resignation from the U.S. Senate. He was succeeded by William A. Graham, who was the 1852 Whig nominee for Vice President on the Winfield Scott ticket. In 1864 Graham was elected to the Confederate senate, and he was elected to the U.S. Senate in 1866, but as a former senior officer of the confederacy, he was forbidden to take his seat.

One other wrinkle of instructions was that they did not necessarily relate to the topic they allegedly addressed. Frequently their purpose was to force a Senator out of office by impaling him on the horns of a dilemma; either do what the instruction meeting wants even if it goes against a public policy to which you have long been committed or be backed into a corner, forced to resign. Thereby instruction became a partisan tool rather than an expression of direct democracy. In fact it could be used as a way to keep running an election campaign again and again if instructors were dissatisfied with the outcome.

As we shall momentarily see, in Lincoln's time public officials and ordinary citizens alike were familiar with the now-forgotten doctrine of instruction. Public officials were answerable for their opinions on a wide range of topics.

Generally instructions' usage did not involve large questions of state. Indeed, on major issues, lack of instructions could be used to sidestep taking a stand. For example, regarding the Compromise of 1850, one senator in Washington declared "this question had not been canvassed before his constituents before he left home, and he was somewhat taken by surprise to find its discussion here."[22]

As we shall now see, politicians of Lincoln's time viewed instruction as just one tool among many that were used to get what persons wanted and using it was routine. In keeping with that attitude, Rep. Thomas Smith (D–IN) "asked the general consent of the House to permit him to lay before the House a number of joint resolutions and memorials which he had been for a long time receiving from his Legislature on a variety of subjects." Permission was denied.[23] No big deal.

Instruction and Its Role in Ratifying U.S. Constitution

Instruction had been accepted as a factor in approving the Articles of Confederation in the 1770s, the first national government of the United States. Georgia's delegate to the Articles' ratification meeting said that "he had not received any instructions from his constituents respecting the Articles of Confederation; but that, his state, having shown so much readiness to ratify them … he had no doubt of their agreeing to the Articles as they stood."[24] Maryland instructed its delegates in Congress to vote for American independence; the September 1776 constitution of Pennsylvania declared, "The people have a right … to instruct their representatives."[25] Indeed the New York state legislature assembled that state's delegation to the Constitutional Convention via instruction.[26] The doctrine was familiar to writers of the U.S. Constitution also. Although some supporters of the Constitution saw conflict between its provisions and the custom of instruction, some

Part 1. Instruction

viewed instruction as a way to resolve complaints about the Philadelphia document. One speaker argued, "If we should ratify the Constitution and *instruct* our first members to Congress, &c. &c, is there not the highest probability that every thing which we wish may be effectually assured?" Another attender of the ratification assembly withdrew his opposition to the Constitution, "especially as the amendments were to be a *standing instruction* to their delegates, until they were obtained, gave it his unreserved assent."[27] Along that line Alexander Hamilton told Rufus King, "This is a reference to the action taken by the Massachusetts legislature on a resolution adopted by the Virginia legislature on December 12, 1795. The Virginia resolution reads: '*Resolved*, That the Senators representing this state in the Senate of the United States, be, and they are hereby instructed, and the Representatives requested to unite their utmost exertions, to obtain in their respective Houses, the following amendments to the Constitution, viz.'"[28] Thomas Jefferson told a correspondent, "Many of the delegates came instructed and determined to vote against it. The discussions brought them over to the side of the Constitution. But they could not vote against their instructions. They therefore asked an adjournment that they might go back to their constituents and ask a repeal of their instructions. Little doubt is entertained that they will accede."[29]

At the New York ratification meeting Alexander Hamilton spoke of the Great Compromise placed in the Philadelphia document, which resulted in a bicameral Congress having a Senate with equal representation for each state and a House membership based on size of state populations. "It will be the interest of the large *states* to increase the representation. This will be the *standing instruction* to their delegates."[30] Also, "if the general voice of the people be for an increase, it undoubtedly must take place. They have it in their power *to instruct their Representatives;* and the state legislatures, *which appoint the Senators* may *enjoin* it also upon them." John Jay told New York listeners, "The Senate is to be composed of men appointed by the state legislatures.... I presume they [state legislatures] will also *instruct them*; ... that there will be a *constant correspondence* supported between the Senators and the *state executive*."[31] The proposed declaration of

Senators Beholden to the People

rights developed at the New York convention called to ratify the Constitution stated, "The people have a right ... to instruct their representatives," and the people "have it in their power to instruct their representatives; and the state legislatures, which appoint the Senators, may enjoin it also upon them."[32] Rhode Islanders debating the Constitution maintained "people have a right peaceably to assemble together, to consult for their common good, or to instruct their representatives."[33] Same at the Vermont ratification meeting: "The people have a right ... to instruct their representatives."[34] Even advocates of the new federal government such as Alexander Hamilton supported instruction in some situations.[35] With similar language across the country, instruction applied to Territorial governments as well as to state governments. The 1836 Arkansas Territorial government's constitution declared that "citizens have a right in a peaceable manner to assemble together for their common good, to instruct their representatives, and to apply to those invested with the power of the government for redress of grievances." The 1849 California territorial constitution said "the people shall have the right freely to assemble together to consult for the common good, to instruct their representatives, and to petition the legislature for redress of grievances." In the 1840s Florida Territory's constitution stated "the people shall have the right to assemble together to consult for the common good, to instruct their representatives, and to petition the Legislature for redress of grievances." In 1859 the Kansas Territory constitution said "the people have a right to assemble, in a peaceable manner, to consult for their common good, to instruct their Representatives, and to petition the Government, or any department thereof, for the redress of grievances." In the Northeast, residents of Maine Territory had a constitution saying, "The people have a right, at all times, in an orderly and peaceable manner, to assemble and consult upon the common good, to give instructions to their representatives, and to request of either department of the government, by petition or remonstrance, redress of their wrongs and grievances." Such guarantees were found in organized territory in the Northwest as well. Michigan Territory had a constitution declaring, "The people have a right, at all times, in

Part 1. Instruction

an orderly and peaceable manner, to assemble and consult upon the common good, to give instructions to their representatives, and to request of either department of the government, by petition or remonstrance, redress of their wrongs and grievances." We find such pledges before and after the Civil War: Ohio 1851 ("The people have a right to assemble together in a peaceable manner to consult for their common good, to instruct their representatives, and to apply to the legislature for redress of grievances") and North Carolina 1868 ("The people have a right to assemble together to consult for their common good, to instruct their representatives, and to apply to the legislature for redress of grievances").

Instruction and Civil Liberties

In the fifteenth article of North Carolina's bill of rights[36] and in North Carolina's ratification of the Constitution,[37] it is stated that "the people have a right peaceably to assemble together to consult for the common good, or to instruct their representatives,"[38] and in North Carolina's first constitution, it is said that "the people have a right to assemble together, to consult for their common good, to instruct their Representatives." Such feelings were not limited to the South. In 1780 a meeting developed the Massachusetts Declaration of Rights (drafted by John Adams), which said in part, "XIX. The people have a right, in an orderly and peaceable manner, to assemble to consult upon the common good; give instructions to their representatives." The first constitution of Massachusetts stated, "The people have a right, in an orderly and peaceable manner, to assemble to consult upon the common good; give instructions to their representatives." Pennsylvania's first constitution declared the same: "The people have a right to assemble together, to consult for their common good, to instruct their representatives." Vermont's first constitution noted "the people have a right to assemble together, to consult for their common good—to instruct their representatives." Instruction was linked to free speech. Thomas Jefferson defended instruction. The Founding Fathers recognized that ability to complain about a government action wasn't the same as being able to do anything about it. The U.S. Constitution's protection of free speech is notable for its silence about instruction. At the first meeting of Congress under the Constitution, in the House of Representatives Congressmen debated whether instruction should be included in the Constitution.[39] The debate demonstrated that the statesmen had much practical experience with instruction despite some theoretical objections.

Rep. Thomas Tudor Tucker of South Carolina noted that Massachusetts had long had a right of instruction and that North Carolina and Virginia recommended that the new Constitution explicitly guarantee that Americans have a right to instruct their Congressmen.[40] Rep. Thomas Hartley of Pennsylvania argued that the right was superfluous, as voters could already remove congressmen at the next election. Pennsylvania's first constitution was less trusting about Hartley's colleagues, declaring "the people have a right to assemble together, to consult for their common good, to instruct their representatives." Hartley also maintained Congressmen were naturally more informed about issues than were members of an instruction meeting and should not be bound by a local group lacking the broad swath of information that Congressmen acquire. He predicted (accurately) that instruction would become a tool of political parties. Tucker also noted that instruction would hinder normal legislative compromises.[41]

As the House discussion continued, Rep. John Page of Virginia stated, "The people have a right to consult for the common good; but to what end will this be done, if they have not the power of instructing their representatives? Instruction and representation in a republic appear to me to be inseparably connected."[42]

Rep. George Clymer of Pennsylvania worried that when voters instructed "they prevent men of abilities and experience from rendering those services to the community ... rendering Congress a mere passive machine."[43]

Speaking to his colleagues Rep. John Sherman of New Hampshire objected that if they "were to be guided by instructions, there would be no use to deliberation; all that a man would have to do, would be to produce his instructions, and lay them on the table, and let them speak for him."[44]

In floor debate Rep. Elbridge Gerry, who was no neophyte to political skullduggery, said Congressmen "will admit an additional check [instruction] against abuses which this, like every other Government, is subject to. Instruction from the people will furnish this in a considerable degree."[45]

Confederate States' Usage of Instruction

Leaders of the Confederate rebellion against the United States had the same heritage of government values as did the rest of the United States. We would expect to see the instruction doctrine to have as much use in the South during the war as the South had in prior times. I'm unaware of convenient documentation of Confederate instruction, but I suspect the following is typical.

> An Ordinance
> In relation to a union of the State of Texas with the Confederate States of America.
> March 22, 1861
> The People of Texas, in convention assembled, have ordained and declared, and do hereby ordain and declare, that the delegation aforesaid, to the Congress aforesaid, be, and they are hereby instructed, and we do accordingly instruct them, in behalf of the State, and as representing its sovereign authority, to apply for the admission of this State into said Confederacy.[46]

State and Local Use of Instruction

The custom became so prevalent that stump speaking by a local politician evolved into meetings of instruction where his audience became his boss. Depending on circumstances, a physical meeting might be dispensed with and the instructions delivered by petition. Elected officeholders pledged themselves to obey instructions from the citizenry. As a public meeting in Plainfield, Illinois, declared: "We

Senators Beholden to the People

hold it to be a fundamental principle of our government, that when a representative cannot obey the will of his constituents, it is his duty to resign, and no man is worthy to represent a free people who will refuse so to do."[47] John Hardin, an Illinois Whig party competitor of Abraham Lincoln, concurred: "I avowed myself the advocate of the republican doctrine of the 'right of instruction,' and have often stated that it was the duty of the representative to obey the will of his constituents."[48]

State legislators expected to be instructed; indeed, the right was guaranteed in the Illinois constitution of 1818: "The people have a right to assemble together in a peaceable manner to consult for their common good, to instruct their representatives, and to apply to the general assembly for redress of grievances."

State representative Abraham Lincoln had enough support that he could evade instructions. For example, constituents wanting to alter a state road's route sent Lincoln a petition, which he acknowledged he would have to obey under the right of instruction. He didn't want to change the route, however, as he had run it to adjoin a friend's farm—a convenience that would also increase the farm's value. The friend was John McNamar, who was once engaged to Lincoln's heartthrob Ann Rutledge. Lincoln's plan required swift action. Lincoln told McNamar to get up a remonstrance against changing the route and to send it to Lincoln immediately. That way Lincoln would have two contradictory sets of instructions, allowing him to choose between them.

Soon after Illinois held its summer 1836 election, agitation began promoting a large (and financially disastrous) public works program, called infrastructure in a later era. An Illinois writer declared if citizens "come not forth in strongest resolutions to the immediate construction of contemplated internal improvements, they are unworthy a heritage in Illinois."[49] During the 1836 Illinois election campaign, in counties across the state, meetings instructed state legislators about general internal improvements and about projects of particular local interest. These meetings continued into autumn. Finally a convention about the topic was called to meet in the state capital just before the next session of the legislature convened. Promoters gathered there and

Part 1. Instruction

agreed on a united front with resolutions delivered to the state legislature. These would be a grand instruction to the entire legislature, superseding local meeting instructions.

State representative John Hardin was one of the few rebels and spoke contemptuously of instructions from "little knots of some ten or twenty speculators who would meet in some flourishing town or city which only existed on paper. I knew ... that the real bone and sinew of the country—those who would have to foot the bill, were not in favor" of this internal improvements system.[50] State representative John McClernand declared to the world that he "was satisfied that not only the people of his own county would sanction its adoption, but the community at large were in favor of it."[51] After the infrastructure system prostrated state finances, however, McClernand publicly claimed he had opposed the project but reluctantly voted for it in obedience to instructions from his constituents.[52] After things went bad state representative James Ralston used the instructions excuse even though he voted five days before instructions arrived.[53] State representative Stephen Douglas took the same approach, saying he worked for the system under instruction from constituents. The instruction Douglas said he was compelled to obey was actually

John Hardin was a member of Congress from Illinois and a Whig party competitor of Abraham Lincoln. Hardin "avowed myself the advocate of the republican doctrine of the 'right of instruction,' and have often stated that it was the duty of the representative to obey the will of his constituents" (*McClure's*, May 1896, Wikimedia Commons).

four different petitions having a total of 156 signatures (the August 1836 election had polled 3,600 votes in the same constituency). Douglas voted against a referendum allowing the people to authorize or forbid the internal improvements system. This was a stance not required by instructions and was arguably intended to prevent public control of a decision. When the internal improvement system was vetoed, Douglas organized a veto override in both houses of the legislature, leadership going far beyond constituent instructions to vote for the system.[54]

So we see that instructions could be a way to escape accountability even though they are usually described as a way for officeholders to be held more accountable for their actions.

Illinois politician Stephen A. Douglas (Library of Congress).

Instructions Promote Continuous Election Campaigns

In 1834 voters in the Cincinnati congressional district of Rep. Robert Lytle (D–OH) irked him with the unusual approach of sending this House member an instruction rather than a request. Regardless of exact vocabulary Lytle described it as an instruction, and his characterization is accepted here. District voters demanded that Lytle work against Jackson's bank policies. The Congressman said he supported the doctrine of instruction, but in this case, "I cannot

Part 1. Instruction

and will not obey." Lytle said that not only were district instructors a minority of voters (700 voters out of 10,000), but they were largely his political opponents who simply wanted to resume an election campaign they had lost. His opponents included "boards of trade, chambers of commerce, counting-house establishments, stock-jobbing associations" and other financial operators.[55] His opposition toward wealthy interests and support for President Andrew Jackson's "common man" policies did not extend to all humble Americans; Lytle promoted race riots against African Americans.

Dispute about President Jackson's national banking policies resulted in the U.S. Senate censuring him for his conduct. In March of 1836 U.S. Senator Thomas Morris (D–OH) presented a resolution from the Ohio general assembly instructing both of the state's U.S. Senators to seek expunging (removal) from the U.S. Senate *Journal* of the Anti-Jackson censure motion. Earlier the Ohio general assembly had passed resolutions instructing Ohio's two senators to support Jackson's bank policies. With sarcastic rhetoric Morris professed confusion about the general assembly's stance and that of Sen. Thomas Ewing (W–OH). Morris then changed to a serious tone. "Disobedience by a Senator to the instructions and requirements of his state as expressed by her legislature is a deep and festering wound…. It gives the Senator for the time being, all the attributes of despotism, the full and free exercise of his own will and authority without accountability." Morris noted that in January 1836 a convention of 500 Ohio Jacksonians from sixty counties unanimously declared,

> We regard the right of instruction as the sheet anchor, the main pillar of our freedom, and … stand by it…. It is only by the frequent and rigid exercise of this invaluable privilege that the democratic character of this Government can be preserved, we believe the agent who disobeys to be unworthy the confidence of his constituents, and that he ought to resign his seat.[56]

In 1835 and again in 1836 the New Hampshire legislature instructed the state's two Senators (Democrats Henry Hubbard and Isaac Hill) to expunge from the Senate *Journal* the censure resolution against President Jackson.[57] Sen. Silas Wright presented "certain resolutions of the Legislature of New York instructing their Senators to support Mr. [Thomas Hart] Benton's expunging resolutions." (More about the expunging resolutions shortly.) Sen. John Clayton (W–DE) "was instructed by his state legislature to vote against these expunging resolutions."[58] Note that the "instructing" pro and con here reflected the party allegiance of the state legislature and of the U.S. Senators; they were being told to do what they already wanted to do.

During Abraham Lincoln's campaign to be elected U.S. Senator by the Illinois general assembly in 1855 (of which we shall hear more in this book), his political allies watched everything. An informant wrote to him, "Our people here are all for you, and if necessary we can get up a public meeting, to instruct our [state] senators and representatives" to support Lincoln.[59] When time arrived in winter 1855 for the legislature to elect a U.S. Senator, an aide to Lincoln's rival Stephen Douglas wrote that "instructions to the [state] senators must be of the right sort."[60]

This was a delicate situation because the eventual winner, Lyman Trumbull, was a Democrat but a leader of the anti–Douglas faction of Illinois Democrats. Douglas's allies relished the prospect of sending embarrassing instructions to Trumbull from the Illinois state capital. In the 1856 presidential election Democrat James Buchanan won a plurality in Illinois but failed to win a majority. Illinois Republicans lamely argued that therefore any instructions to Trumbull from Democrats allied with Douglas or Buchanan were invalid and Trumbull could disregard them. Not the most compelling argument, but at least it demonstrated that instructions were taken seriously. Trumbull couldn't just ignore them.

The defeated candidate Abraham Lincoln was another player in the instruction game. Douglas was sweating a possibility of the Illinois legislature telling him to seek restoration of the Missouri Compromise that Douglas had been fighting against. Indeed, Lincoln was drafting such instructions and got Lincoln supporters to submit them to the state legislature. His instructions not only required Douglas to work at restoring the Missouri Compromise. In addition he had to

Part 1. Instruction

prevent the Territories of Kansas and Nebraska from being admitted to the Union as slave states, prevent extension of slavery into anyplace currently free, and maintain the illegality of the African slave trade.[61] Douglas was scheming a way to label such instructions as invalid and thereby not binding on him. He couldn't simply ignore Lincoln's plotting. Said Douglas, "Any vote which I have given, or may give, inconsistent with [my] principle, will be the vote of those who gave the instructions, and not my own."[62] Sen. Hannibal Hamlin (D–ME) "presented a resolution of the legislature of Maine, instructing the Senators and requesting the Representatives of that state to oppose the passage of the Nebraska bill so long as it shall contain any provision repealing, abrogating rescinding, or in any way invalidating the Missouri Compromise."[63]

Illinois politician Lyman Trumbull (Library of Congress).

To see more about how instruction operated, let us now examine a few specific issues of the nineteenth century.

Banking

As the War of 1812 approached, a question arose about whether the charter of the private Bank of the United States should be renewed. Many Americans suspected bankers of engaging in crooked conduct, but financiers argued that the BUS was needed to help raise money for national defense. Young Virginia legislator Benjamin Watkins Leigh (whose political identification was in flux) wrote resolutions containing instructions for Virginia's U.S. Senators to oppose rechartering the bank. U.S. Senator Richard Brent disobeyed and voted to recharter. Virginia's other U.S. Senator, William Branch Giles, obeyed but declared he did not recognize the validity of instruction.

In the 1830s arguments about banking were among the larger controversies in American politics. One of the biggest fights was over President Jackson's removal of federal revenue deposits from the private Bank of the United States. Although the bank was private, it functioned as a national bank that could discipline wildcat banks. Jackson and his supporters viewed BUS as an arm of Henry Clay and his Whig allies who could use BUS to fund Whig operations. Jackson decided to remove federal deposits from BUS and transfer them to banks friendly to Jackson (sometimes called the Independent Treasury Act or Subtreasury Act). The process was a little complex, and several state legislatures, such as Indiana's,[64] and that of Illinois,[65] instructed their U.S Senators to take one stance or another. Technical details need not concern us, but in response, the Whig Party sought to impeach Democratic President Andrew Jackson in March 1834.[66] Whigs had a majority of Senators but not the two-thirds majority required to convict Jackson and remove him from office. Whigs tried a tactic not mentioned in the Constitution, passing a resolution of censure saying: "Resolved that the President in the late Executive proceedings in relation to the public revenue, has assumed upon himself authority and power not conferred by the Constitution and laws, but in derogation of both." From the Whig standpoint this tactic had a few merits: (1) it was something they could do (instead of meeting the impossible arithmetic needed to achieve an impeachment conviction), (2) it would be an action by the same persons who would vote on impeachment (thereby having the moral force of an impeachment conviction even if Jackson was acquitted for lack of a two-thirds majority), and (3) it could prevent Jackson from defending himself against charges laid against him (since censure was a proceeding unrecognized by the Constitution) and Jackson had no right of reply.

Part 1. Instruction

Democrats were enraged by Whig conduct and spent three years trying to reverse the censure vote. In 1835 New York Democratic senator Silas Wright noted that the New York legislature had instructed him and fellow U.S. Senator Nathaniel Tallmadge to support expunging the censure resolution from the Senate *Journal*. Pennsylvania's U.S. Senator Samuel McKean worked with New York Democratic Senator Silas Wright to reconcile instructions that came from one branch of the Pennsylvania legislature. In 1835 Whig Sen. John Clayton refused to accept the Delaware legislature's instructions on reversing the censure vote.[67] Finally, the 1836 election gave Democrats a U.S. Senate majority, and just before Jackson retired from the presidency in March 1837, they voted to expunge the censure resolution from the Senate *Journal*.

This three-year controversy did not go unnoticed by users of instruction. Whigs had a majority in the Virginia state legislature and in February 1834, by a vote of 114 to 14, instructed U.S. Senator William Cabell Rives to criticize Jackson for removing federal deposits from the Bank of the United States and work at restoring those deposits into

Missouri U.S. Senator Thomas Hart Benton was one of President Jackson's staunchest supporters in Congress. After the Whig-led U.S. Senate censured Jackson for his policy regarding the second Bank of the United States, a mountain of instructions, pro and con, arrived on Senators' desks from home states. Eventually Benton masterminded victory for Jackson by passing a resolution expunging the Whig-designed condemnation from the Senate *Journal* (State Historical Society of Missouri, Art Collection 1978.0261).

Bank of the United States. As a Jacksonian, Rives declined to do the Whigs' bidding and instead resigned from the Senate. In February 1836 Virginia's U.S. Senator John Tyler, whose political loyalties were uncertain, took the same approach, resigning rather than obey the Virginia legislature. The Whig general assembly could then replace them, a contest that was more acute than banking policy was.

In 1838 Connecticut's general assembly instructed the state's two Senators, John Niles and Perry Smith, along with requesting the state's U.S. Representatives, to vote against Jackson's banking policies.[68] Smith "of Indiana presented a resolution of the general assembly of his state, instructing their Senators and Representatives 'to procure, if possible, by their exertions, at as early a day as may be in their power, a repeal of a bill passed at the last session of Congress, known as the Independent Treasury bill'"[69] (the opposite of what the legislature of the next-door state of Illinois was instructing its congressional delegation to do).

In 1841 the Maine legislature instructed Sen. William Fessenden to oppose Jackson's banking policy,[70] and after passing resolutions against Jackson's banking policies, Maine's legislature declared, "The Hon. Reuel Williams, previous to his election to the Senate of the United States, having declared and published that it is the duty of the elected to carry into effect the will of his constituents, if he is instructed what that will is, or resign his trust, we, therefore, hereby *instruct him* that the foregoing resolutions express the will of his constituents."[71]

Rejecting the Illinois legislature's anti–Jackson instructions, Sen. John Robinson (D–IL) proclaimed, "My political creed forbids disregard to the legitimate instructions from the body whose voice honored me with a seat here." Robinson said that the voters of Illinois had sent their instructions via their votes in the state election a few months earlier and he did not recognize any change in those instructions that were delivered by that election.[72]

In May 1834 an exasperated U.S. Rep. Gayton Osgood (D–MA) complained about the way a convention of constituents was giving instructions on rechartering the Bank of the United States and restoring federal deposits to the institution.

Part 1. Instruction

If ... a part of my constituents, or a majority, if you please, had undertaken to instruct me to vote for a recharter of the bank ... might I not have turned round upon them and said, a year has not yet elapsed since you elected me with a knowledge that I should vote against the bank, and now you instruct me to vote for it? How long must I suppose that these your new instructions will remain valid? Have I any assurance that you will not change your minds again before the vote is taken? And if you do, must I change with you? Must I veer about with every current of wind that happens to strike the political weathercock in my district?[73]

In January 1835 Democrat U.S. Senator William R. King of Alabama brought resolutions to the Senate from Alabama, instructing the state's two Senators to support Jackson's bank policies or else resign. King said he felt obligated to obey. Alabama's other Senator, Democrat Gabriel Moore (D–AL), sounded just as exasperated with Alabama's general assembly, which instructed him to resign and then to support expunging Jackson's censure from the Senate *Journal* (a neat trick if you were no longer a Senator). Although Moore had supported instruction in principle, he now held that the state's general assembly lacked power to alter his tenure of office. Unfortunately for Moore he squabbled with future President Martin Van Buren who was close to General Jackson. The general promoted meetings of Moore opponents in Alabama. When the Alabama meetings instructed Moore to resign he refused to do so and was defeated in every subsequent effort to win elective office.

U.S. Senator Isaac Hill (D–NH) handled resolutions forwarded to him from the state legislature calling on Whig U.S. Senator Samuel Bell to resign for lack of candor and also instructions for both Senators to support expunging the U.S. Senate's censure of Jackson. Bell retained office but did not seek reelection to the Senate.

On the U.S. Senate floor Senator Young of Illinois presented resolutions from the Illinois general assembly instructing the state's two Senators "to use their exertions to prevent the repeal of the Independent Treasury [subtreasury] law; and vote against all bills having for their object the establishment of a national bank."[74]

Joseph C. Guild was a Tennessee legislator who had been a lieutenant colonel fighting against Indians in the Seminole War, a conflict supported by President Jackson. Guild introduced measures requiring Tennessee's two U.S. Senators to vote in favor of expunging the censure resolution. Jackson promoted meetings across the state calling on the Tennessee legislature to instruct its senators, Hugh White and Ephraim H. Foster, to support expunging the censure resolution. In addition to some personal lobbying by Jackson, Martin Van Buren mailed to Tennessee legislators copies of Sen. Thomas Hart Benton's oration calling for expunging the censure resolution. White had formerly been a Jackson supporter but was now a Whig candidate for President and resigned from the Senate rather than submit. Foster, too, resigned rather than disobey. Whigs took control of the Tennessee state legislature and elected Jackson's friend Felix Grundy to the U.S. Senate with the intention of instructing him to oppose Jackson's banking policies, particularly the subtreasury policy that would deposit federal revenue in the U.S. Treasury Department rather than in private banks. In theory this situation would force Jackson loyalist Grundy to resign rather than vote against Jackson's subtreasury plan in the Senate, but "Mr. Grundy rose and remarked, that he had risen to present to the Senate a preamble and resolutions adopted by the general assembly of the state of Tennessee. By one of these resolutions, the Senators are positively instructed, and the Representatives in Congress from the state are requested, 'to vote against any law which may propose to enforce the Sub-Treasury system of finance recommended by the President of the United States in his message to Congress.'" Grundy refused to be intimidated and refused to resign.[75]

Senators had a good feel for what state legislators and the voters at large would tolerate, and instances existed where Senators successfully defied instructions.[76] Instructions were twice violated by Sen. Gideon Tomlinson, and he was nominated for reelection in 1836 and 1837.[77] In January 1834 the New Jersey legislature instructed Sen. Theodore Frelinghuysen and the other New Jersey Senator, Samuel Southard, to oppose President Jackson's banking policy, especially removal of federal deposits from the Bank of the United States. The New Jersey legislature wanted those deposits restored. Frelinghuysen declared he generally supported the right of instruction, but Jackson's bank policy

Part 1. Instruction

was correct, and he refused to resign. Frelinghuysen said he was confident that voters would sustain his stance.

Saying that someone had to stand up to Jackson, in 1836 U.S. Senator Willie P. Mangum resigned rather than accept the North Carolina legislature's instruction to support Jackson's bank policy. He had already disobeyed the legislature's instructions the previous year, so his stance in 1836 was not hard to predict. Delaware's Whig leader Sen. John Middleton Clayton received anti–Jackson instructions.[78]

Different states had different approaches to slavery, and these approaches were reflected by instructions that state legislatures gave to U.S. Senators.

Instruction was a way to bring up topics that Congress did not want to discuss. For example, in 1839 Senator Samuel Prentiss "presented certain resolutions from the legislature of the state of Vermont, instructing their Senators ... to use their efforts to prevent the passage of any law for the annexation of Texas to the Union, and to procure the passage of law for the abolition of slavery and the slave trade in the District of Columbia and the Territories of the Union, and of the slave trade between the several states."[79] These resolutions pre-dated the Mexican War. In contrast the Mississippi legislature instructed Senators to help annex Texas.[80] Typical Texas settlers, who included relatives of John Hardin (an Illinois Whig competitor of Lincoln), were known to be slavery proponents.

A long-standing dispute sidetracked anti-slavery petitions received by Congress. Prentiss noted "the virtual rejection of petitions here was regarded as an infraction of the right of petition." He added, "These resolutions were passed by the legislature of Vermont in consequence of petitions requiring their passage." Note the double layer of instructions. Meetings of voters in Vermont instructed the state legislature, which in turn instructed members of the state's congressional delegation. Angry slaveholder aristocrats in the Senate chamber immediately protested. Prentiss professed shock that such resolutions would offend the Southerners. Prentiss "said he had made the motion to print these resolutions because he supposed it would be an act of proper courtesy to the legislature from whom they come."[81] I doubt that his professed surprise was genuine, but he did demonstrate a creative use of instructions.

Some state legislators sought ways to reduce sectional conflict by answering the question, "If emancipation occurred, where were free blacks going to live?" Instructions provided some possibilities to consider. The Ohio general assembly instructed the state's two Senators to "inquire into the expediency of enacting a law setting apart a portion of the newly acquired [Mexican] territory for the benefit of such free persons as may become setters thereon."[82] A few weeks later the same legislature instructed their U.S. Senators "to inquire into the expediency of procuring the passage of a law authorizing the survey, and appropriation of a portion of the territory acquired from Mexico, for the benefit of all free persons of color who become actual settlers, and to establish schools for them."[83]

After helping to design and pass the Compromise of 1850, Douglas gave a floor speech explaining his absence at a crucial moment.

> The legislature of Illinois had passed a resolution instructing me to vote for a bill for the government of the territory acquired from Mexico, which should contain an express prohibition of slavery in that territory while it remained as territories [sic], leaving the people to do as they pleased [about becoming a slave state] when they become a state. The instruction was designed in order to compel me to resign my seat and give place to a Freesoiler. The legislature knew my inflexible opposition to the principles asserted in the instructions.... I wrote the bills and reported them from the Committee on Territories without the prohibition, in order that the record might show what my opinions were.... A Freesoil Senator offered an amendment in the language of my instructions. I knew that the amendment could not prevail, even if the vote of Illinois was recorded in its favor.... Duty required me to retain my seat. I was prepared to fight and defy abolitionism in all its forms, but I was not willing to repudiate the settled doctrine of my State, in regard to the right of instruction.... Any vote which might be recorded in my name seemingly in its favor, would be the vote of those who gave the instructions., and not my own.... A few weeks afterward the legislature of Illinois assembled, and one of its first acts was to repeal the resolutions of instructions to which I have referred.[84]

U.S. Sen. Jacob Miller, Whig of New Jersey, delivered a soothing resolution from the state legislature "that our Senators and

Part 1. Instruction

Representatives in Congress are hereby requested to vote on all questions of a sectional character consistent with a rigid construction of the Constitution, as will have a tendency to allay any geographical animosities which may exist, and promote the same harmony in our national councils."[85] (Note the term "requested" here applied to a U.S Senator instead of the command "instruct." This usage is evidence that the issue was of lower concern to the New Jersey legislature than were other sectional controversies.) Senators had a good sense of how far they could push groups that were instructing them. Sen. Moses MacDonald said, "The legislature of Maine did not propose to instruct him to vote against [Douglas's Nebraska] ... bill, but put forth a modest request to that effect. But he did not intend to carry out their wishes, that body not properly representing public sentiment in that State."[86]

In contrast the Missouri general assembly instructed Sen. David Atchison and Sen. Thomas Hart Benton to oppose "any attempt ... to legislate on the subject so as to affect the institution of slavery in the States, in the District of Columbia, or in the Territories is, to say the least, a violation of the principle upon which that instrument [U.S. Constitution] was founded." And "any organization of the Territorial governments excluding the citizens of any part of the Union from removing to such Territories with their property [i.e., slaveholders bringing their chattels]" would violate the Constitution's spirit. In the Southern view, actions of Northern states had broken the Missouri Compromise of 1820. Missouri held that the status of slavery in Territories must be determined by residents thereof. "Passage of any act conflicting with the principles herein expressed, Missouri will be found in hearty cooperation with the slaveholding States in such measures as may be deemed necessary for our mutual protection against the encroachments of Northern fanaticism."[87] In March of 1840 the Georgia legislature instructed its U.S. Senators to seek tightening of federal laws protecting rights of slave owners.[88] "Showing friendliness to the Southern slaveocracy, in 1836 Connecticut's general assembly instructed the state's U.S. Senators to recognize the independence of Texas,"[89] which was a friendly environment for slavery.

Instruction cropped up routinely in political conversation. An oddball competition, almost, broke out in Senate floor debate about the Wilmot Proviso, which banned slavery in territory acquired when the United States prevailed in the Mexican War. Senators argued about who had the most support from state legislatures about the Proviso bill. Whig New York Senator William Seward declared, "I have no recollection that I have at any time stated in the Senate that there are fifteen or any other number of state legislatures which have instructed their representatives to vote for the Wilmot Proviso."[90]

Despite the huge vote sent by the instructing state legislature (133 to 3), Cameron had little concern about the issue. "He said that for the first time he was called upon to give a vote not the result of his own reflection. He digressed briefly to give his opinion upon the responsibility of obeying instructions from the state legislatures."

> He was free to say that he would not obey instructions not in accordance with the opinions and wishes of the people who elected the legislature giving them; or if they should instruct him to do an act which subsequent information should convince him they had adopted upon wrong information, he would not hesitate to take the responsibility of disobeying them, and would rely with confidence on the purity of his intentions and the result of his vote as his justification with the people, who were the common masters of all representatives. But upon a question on which public opinion was clear, he should never hesitate, and would cheerfully obey—for, in his opinion no principle was more clear than the agent was bound to carry out in good faith the wishes of his principal. So clear was he on the subject, that he would never hesitate to give up his own opinion, and adopt that which he knew to be the decided opinion of his state.

From the other angle on the slavery question, in 1850 Vermont's general assembly requested (rather than instructed) its U.S. Senators to resist expanding slave territory, to ban slavery in the District of Columbia, and to apply the Wilmot Proviso's ban against slavery to new territory acquired by the United States.[91] Vermont's state legislature instructed its two Senators to ban the sea-going slave trade from international waters and establish New Mexico and California as free territory. Michigan's legislature instructed the two Senators to work for admission of California to the Union without delay.[92] Sen. Isaac

Part 1. Instruction

Toucey "made a few remarks, in which he said he should not obey the instructions of the Whig abolition legislature of Connecticut, as to the vote he should give on this [Nebraska] bill."[93]

One of the greatest political disputes of this era was the decision by Sen. Stephen Douglas to repeal the Missouri Compromise via the Kansas–Nebraska Act, also referred to as the Nebraska Bill. The Georgia and Mississippi legislatures instructed their Senators to work for Douglas's Nebraska bill and its principles.[94] Those principles included making Kansas a slave state under the so-called Lecompton constitution, an action which Tennessee's legislature instructed Sen. John Bell to do.[95] Bell sidestepped the instruction, a shuffle that Senator (and future President) Andrew Johnson (D–TN) caught and protested.[96]

The New York general assembly requested the state's U.S. Senators to fight against repeal of Missouri Compromise.[97] A month or two thereafter U.S. Rep. Henry Bennett of New York declared on the House floor:

> An article appeared in the *Washington Union* on Saturday last, in relation to my colleague, [John Taylor] in which it is stated that he had avowed his determination to vote for the Nebraska bill. I have received a large petition against this bill from the county of Tioga, where my colleague resides, ... signed by, I think, over one thousand citizens, with a request to present it in the House.... The petition was accompanied with a statement that it was designed as an instruction to my colleague to vote against the Nebraska bill, and that he had declared, in a public meeting, in that county, that he would vote against the Nebraska bill or resign, and signifying their request to have him do so.[98]

Maine Democratic Senator Hannibal Hamlin "presented a resolution of the legislature of Maine, instructing the Senators and requesting the Representatives of that state to oppose the passage of the Kansas-Nebraska bill so long as it shall contain any provision repealing, abrogating, rescinding, or in any invalidating the Missouri Compromise."[99]

In 1854, when Abraham Lincoln stumped the state of Illinois condemning the legislative effort Stephen Douglas was making to expand slave territory via the Nebraska bill, Lincoln told crowds, "If this state should instruct Douglas to vote for the repeal of the ... bill, he

[Douglas] must do it, for 'the doctrine of instruction' was part of his political creed."[100]

Transportation

In Lincoln's time members of Congress were considered gatekeepers of federal money available for assorted business projects and could be instructed to unlock the gate. Among the most common desires was funding that would improve a wide variety of transportation.

In 1836 the Missouri legislature instructed the two Senators and requested the state's Representatives "to use their influence to obtain appropriations for the improvement of the navigation of the Missouri and Mississippi rivers."[101] Later the Pennsylvania general assembly instructed Senators to seek congressional funding for improving the Ohio River,[102] and the Indiana legislature did the same.[103]

Sen. Robert Walker presented a preamble and resolutions from the legislature of Mississippi, "instructing Senators to use and requesting Representatives to use their best exertions to procure the passage of a law to regulate and improve the steamboat navigation."[104]

Mississippi's legislature instructed Senators to seek construction of a lighthouse between Mobile Bay and Pearl River,[105] and the New Jersey general assembly requested Senators to get "an appropriation for ... constructing a light-house on Absecom beach, and anchoring a bell buoy outside of Absecom bar." Also the New Jersey legislature requested Senators get an appropriation for construction of "a breakwater at Cape May."[106]

Railroads were the coming thing in land transportation and both private entrepreneurs and state governments sought congressional aid. In 1840 Senator Young of Illinois "presented a preamble and resolution passed by the General Assembly of Illinois, instructing the Senators and requesting the Representatives of said state in Congress to use their exertions to procure the passage of an act granting to that state, for public improvements, each alternate section [of land] on the different routes in Illinois, or the whole of the unsold public lands lying within her limits, on condition that one-third the proceeds of the sales thereof should be paid to the General [federal] Government."[107]

Such a funding scheme is associated with the transcontinental railway but (as we can see) was proposed far earlier.

Sen. Samuel McKean "presented resolutions passed by the legislature of Pennsylvania, requesting their Senators and Representatives in Congress to vote for, and use their best exertions to obtain, the passage of a law authorizing the construction of a macadamized road from the National road, at some suitable point west of the western base of Laurel Hill, by way of the United States arsenal near Pittsburg and the state arsenal at Meadville, to the harbor of Erie, and appropriating a sufficient sum of money out of the Treasury of the United States for its immediate construction and speedy completion."[108]

The main form of land transportation omitted from attempts to receive money from Congress was canal development, perhaps an indication that its time was fading. Still, water was portrayed as a more democratic method of transportation than railroads. Anyone could ship via canal or river, whereas a railroad required a car to be rented from the railway.

Public Land

There is a reason for the invention of the phrase that something is "doing a land office business."

Public land was free money, costing the government nothing to produce. The federal government acted virtually like a twenty-first-century charitable foundation, looking for likely recipients. Settlers and speculators alike sought real estate from the federal government. Sometimes the property was used in lieu of cash, by government (such as land bounties given for military service) and by recipients (such as comprising the endowment of land grant colleges). Westerners tended to want cheap land and plenty of it. Eastern capitalists preferred to throw roadblocks against people who could escape unfair labor politics by moving West. A further wrinkle was that public land policy was linked to President Jackson's banking policy, with Whig Sen. Henry Clay seeking to distribute surplus federal receipts to states (called "revenue sharing" in a later era). The policy was just as controversial in the 1830s as it was in the 1970s.[109] The legislature of Mississippi instructed Senators to seek repeal of distribution act[110] and the general assembly of New York instructed Senators to seek repeal of the distribution law.[111]

Land sales were among chief sources of federal income; consequently, slight changes in government regulations could make or break fortunes. Indeed, U.S. Sen. Richard Young "presented resolutions of the legislature of Illinois, instructing their Senators and requesting their Representatives in Congress to use their best exertions to procure the passage of a law making appropriations sufficient to put all the unsurveyed lands of the state under immediate contract."[112]

Many military veterans were entitled to free land as a veterans' benefit. In 1850 the Michigan legislature instructed Senators for "enactment of a law granting compensation in bounty lands, or money, to all commissioned officers in the late war with Mexico below the grade of brigadier-general."[113] That same month the Louisiana legislature instructed the state's two Senators "to use their exertions to procure grants of bounty land to the commissioned officers of the late war with Mexico."[114] Also that same month the Pennsylvania legislature instructed Senators to get a law "granting bounty lands to the officers, soldiers, seamen, and marines of the last war with Great Britain."[115] Civilians, too, received real estate largess from the government. In 1838 Sen. Samuel McKean "presented resolutions of the legislature of Pennsylvania ... setting forth the sufferings and losses of the early settlers of the Wyoming valley, and instructing their Senators and requesting their Representatives to procure, if possible, by their votes and influence, the passage of a law that will compensate the Wyoming sufferers of the Revolution for such losses."[116]

In a straight-up instruction New York required Senators to promote land grants to settlers.[117] The Indiana legislature instructed the state's Senators to "use their influence to procure a donation by Congress of 4,000 acres of land in the Miami Reserve for the use of the Indiana University."[118] How reliable legislatures would be with such

Part 1. Instruction

grants is questionable. For example, the Illinois general assembly instructed the state's two Senators to seek donation of $500,000 of public land to Illinois for scholastic purposes.[119] In the past, however, the Illinois legislature had borrowed from the school fund, conduct that may well have embarrassed the Senators and for sure earned state officials a reputation of undependability.

Sen. Daniel Sturgeon "said he held in his hand resolutions passed by the legislature of Pennsylvania instructing him and his [Senate] colleague James Buchanan to vote for a distribution of the proceeds of the sales of the public lands among the states...." Sturgeon said he would "obey the general tenor of the resolutions." Sturgeon added, "Although he was not among those who had implicit faith in legislative instructions, nor would he yield them implicit obedience, yet while he held a seat in the Senate of the United States, he should feel disposed to conform, in his vote to the wishes of the people of the state of which he had the honor in part to represent; and as he was inclined to believe that a majority of the people of the state of Pennsylvania may be at this time in favor of the distribution of the proceeds of the sales of the public lands, he was disposed to take the resolutions of the legislature as collateral evidence, and collateral evidence alone, of the fact. He should cast his vote accordingly."[120]

Tariff

In addition to public land, tariff receipts were a major part of the federal income. Controversy arose regarding whether the tariff should only be used to generate revenue or whether it should have an additional function of protecting American manufacturing from cheap foreign imports. Democrats tended to favor the revenue approach, Whigs the protectionist position. The Arkansas general assembly unanimously instructed Senators to seek lower tariffs,[121] and Mississippi's legislature instructed Senators to work against discriminatory tariffs.[122] Resolutions of the senate and house of the Pennsylvania legislature instructed Senators and Representatives in Congress to oppose all attempts to change the 1842 tariff.

We have seen that "instruction" was a major element of

Senators Beholden to the People

American democracy in Lincoln's time. Although some states codified instruction, mainly it existed as a custom, demonstrating how powerful tradition can be. So why did such an important part of American government disappear? Part of the reason was that proponents of representative democracy prevailed over advocates of direct democracy. Either method can work, but representative democracy produced results more expeditiously. Instruction simply died out, unable to produce results that representative democracy could produce. Commands such as this one on foreign affairs, dating from 1882, became uncommon:

> Whereas in the execution of the coercive policy now practiced by the British Government in Ireland....
>
> *Resolved,* That our Senators and Representatives in Congress are hereby instructed to use their best efforts to secure as soon as possible such a recognition of the rights of American citizens abroad as will be consistent with our national dignity, and avert future capricious, arbitrary, or unjust interference with them. That copies of the foregoing preamble and resolutions be forwarded immediately to ... our Senators and Representatives in Congress.[123]

In 1911 U.S. Sen. Robert Owen (D–OK) gave a floor speech of interest to us, because although most Progressives of that era were Republicans, Owen was a Democrat. He noted, "From the days of Jefferson as President the right of the people to instruct their Representatives was freely recognized, but gradually the growth of party nominations by the delegate system took the power out of the hands of the people and put it in the hands of the [political] machine men."[124]

As we shall see now, part of instruction's demise was due to a major change in the way that U.S Senators were chosen. In theory the new method was supposed to make government more responsive to the people but the opposite happened.

PART 2

Election of Senators by State Legislatures

One merit of the instruction system is that it proved its serviceability through decades of use. It had drawbacks but largely delivered the goods.

The same could not be said of the Electoral College, which was established for the sole purpose of selecting who would be chosen to serve as President of the United States. Its dismal history is well documented elsewhere, but one aspect deserves mention here.

In Lincoln's time Electors were real people. By that I mean they weren't ciphers. Readers of this book (and its author) would be hard-pressed to name even one Elector who participated in the latest presidential election. Not so in Lincoln's era. He and other leaders of Illinois Whigs met privately to choose Elector candidates, although in a sign of democratization, by 1839 those choices were being ratified at the Whig Party's Illinois state convention. (Later some politicians argued that conventions were less democratic than allowing all members of a political party to vote on who the party's nominee should be. But at least Illinois Whigs were moving in a democratic direction.) Electors were well known politicians who ran a presidential candidate's campaign in a state congressional district. Electors might even serve as a surrogate for the presidential candidate and face an opposing Elector in public debates. An active role for Electors in political campaigns continued into the early twentieth century.

Such gatherings could be massive. On Thursday, June 4, 1840, 15,000 Whigs paraded through Springfield, Illinois, in ranks that

Senators Beholden to the People

stretched two and a half miles. Attendees ate at a barbecue boasting four tables, each 160 feet long. At this 1840 meeting

> Mr. Lincoln stood in a wagon from which he addressed the mass of people that surrounded it.... Much time was devoted to telling stories to illustrate some phase of his argument, though more often the telling of these stories was resorted to for the purpose of rendering his opponents ridiculous.... In that kind of oratory he excelled.... One story he told on that occasion ... was not an impure story, yet it was not one it would be seemly to publish.... The same story might have been told by another in such a way that it would probably have been regarded as transcending the proprieties of popular address ... yet the manner of telling them was so peculiarly his own that they gave no offence even to refined and cultured people. On the contrary, they were much enjoyed. The story he told on this occasion was much liked by the vast assembly that surrounded the temporary platform from which he spoke and was received with loud bursts of laughter and applause.[1]

Moreover, when Lincoln was active in politics, state constitutions were evolving from their traditional provisions giving the governor power to appoint key state officials, such as the attorney general and secretary of state. That choice was becoming a decision made by ordinary voters.

In the previous chapter we examined how the doctrine of instruction worked, with particular emphasis on election of U.S. Senators by state legislatures. We shall now investigate that activity a little deeper and examine how Amendment Seventeen was added to the U.S. Constitution in 1913, transferring election of U.S. Senators from state legislatures to popular election by ordinary voters. The change made U.S. Senators answerable to tens of thousands of voters rather than to a comparative handful of state legislators.

This change of constituencies was a goal of the Progressive political movement, which showed growing strength as the twentieth century began. The expectation was that U.S. Senators elected by the popular vote would be less approachable by big corporations and be more responsive to desires of voters who elected the U.S. Senators. This is not how it turned out.

Under the Seventeenth Amendment the same types of wealthy corporations and individuals gained access to U.S. Senators in the 1990s as

Part 2. Election of Senators by State Legislatures

in the 1890s. Much of the access was ordinary "open doors" to a U.S. Senator's prominent supporters, but there was also the occasional incident of bribery or embezzlement before and after the Seventeenth Amendment. Examples might be appropriate at this point. At the time they occurred they were not common enough to destroy the Senate's credibility, but a few instances went a long way toward poisoning public thought about the Senate's role as a preeminent institution in American life.

The Senate itself issued reports that fueled public outrage. Typically they excused outrageous conduct. Sometimes reports didn't even reveal who was under investigation. Here is an example:

> Resolution. That the Committee on Privileges and Elections are hereby instructed to inquire and report to the Senate whether efforts were made by railway or other corporations, their agents, employees, or others, to control the election to the United States Senate by the Legislature of Florida in the year 1891; whether money and free transportation were used by them or any of them to influence the vote of the people for members of the Legislature, or to influence the votes of the members of the Legislature after their election; whether money was used by combinations of persons made under the influence of agents or persons acting in the interest of corporations to control the election of members of the Legislature and to control their votes after their election; whether newspapers were bought or subsidized by them or by persons acting in their interest or with money obtained either directly or indirectly from them or persons in any way connected with them to oppose the election of some persons and support the election of others; and whether legislation if any, either by an amendment to the Constitution or otherwise, is necessary to protect the people in their right to elect members of the Legislature, who are to choose Senators of the United States, and to protect the members elected from the influences of corporations and their foreign bond-holders. Resolved, That the committee have power to employ a stenographer, and to send for and compel the attendance of witnesses.[2]

Examples of Senatorial Conduct Before the Seventeenth Amendment

The Founding Fathers mistakenly thought that U.S. Senators would not be personally corrupt. Why they thought so is puzzling.

Senators Beholden to the People

Dishonesty in American government of the 1700s was not routine but neither was it unheard of. In fact, sleazy conduct was known virtually from the Senate's beginning.

William Blount

For example, President George Washington appointed William Blount as governor of Southwest Territory, which soon became the state of Tennessee, whose state legislature chose Blount as a U.S. Senator in 1796. Like many government officials of that era Blount decided to speculate in real estate, acquiring millions of acres. A young assistant of his named James Cole Mountflorence described the cession of Tennessee as being tied closely to North Carolina's ratification of the U.S. Constitution. Having served as a delegate from Davidson County, he gave this account of the ratifying convention: "All the delegates from the district of Tennessee were instructed by their constituents to procure, at the same time, a cession of their country to Congress: the Blounts had vast possessions in that district, and therefore felt an equal interest with us in carrying that point in the assembly of the State. The Legislature and the Convention met, in the same month, at Fayetteville: I laboured strenuously, in cooperation with the Blount-interest and with others, to accomplish the wish of my constituents;

U.S. Senator William Blount (New York Public Library).

Part 2. Election of Senators by State Legislatures

our joint efforts were crowned with success, the cession was voted, and I had the honor of being one of those to whom the formation of the Bill, which passed the House to that effect, was intrusted."

This investment by Blount was largely funded with borrowed money. When demand for this property declined, Blount faced ruin. He devised a scheme to recover financially by taking ownership of the port of New Orleans, New Madrid, and Pensacola, with help from the British navy and American militia forces—the latter being under Blount's personal command, with help from Native American allies. Blount was indiscreet enough to explain his plan in writing, which made for interesting reading when intercepted by Secretary of War Pickering and President Adams. In the letter Blount told a fellow conspirator about "the business Captain Chesholm mentioned to the British Minister last winter in Philadelphia." Blount predicted "the plan then talked of will be attempted this fall; and if it is attempted, it will be in a much larger way than then talked of; and if the Indians act their part, I have no doubt but it will succeed." He added, "A man of consequence has gone to England about the business, and if he makes the arrangements as he expects, I shall myself have a hand in the business, and probably shall be at the head of the business on the part of the British."[3]

President Adams's wife Abigail was a shrewd observer of public affairs and wrote to

For an eighteenth-century woman, Abigail Adams was remarkably active politically, keeping up intense and knowledgeable correspondence with her husband John and with women who shared her interest in public affairs. She condemned Sen. William Blount's conduct. This portrait by Benjamin Blyth dates from 1766 (Library of Congress).

Senators Beholden to the People

her sister, "When shall we cease to have Judases? Here is a diabolical plot disclosed ... the letter was read which threw the whole Senate into a consternation.... Corruption is corruption from whatever source it originates. This same Tennessee Senator was arrested for debt four different times on his return home last fall, and but for his privilege as Senator which screens him 20 days, he would have been lodged in Jail."[4] General Washington, who may have felt some embarrassment about aid he had given to Blount's political career, declared that Blount should be "held in detestation by all good men." Washington also stated,

> The intercepted letter ... is really an abomination; disgraceful to the Author; and to be regretted, that among us, a man in high trust, and a responsible station, should be found, so debased in his principles as to write it.... I hope the original letter, if it carries the marks of genuineness, has been carefully preserved and forwarded to the proper departments, that the person guilty of such atrocious conduct may be held to public view in the light he ought to be considered by every honest man, & friend to his Country.

Scene of U.S. Senate debating Blount's impeachment from the Senate (Library of Congress).

Part 2. Election of Senators by State Legislatures

Blount fled from the nation's capital and briefly became a fugitive from justice. He finally faced his peers and was expelled from the Senate after a near-riot on the subject broke out in the Senate chamber. He remained popular in Tennessee and subsequently won election to state office.

Blount's conduct may have influenced Andrew Jackson, who was a U.S. Senator from Tennessee at the time and was one of the immortals who voted against a resolution thanking Washington for service to his country.

Jesse Bright

Jesse Bright (D–IN) was a leader of the Indiana state Democratic party and one of President James Buchanan's prime operatives. In 1854 the *Chicago Daily Tribune* reported that U.S. Senator Stephen Douglas was making a political visit to Chicago and would be accompanied by his colleague from Indiana, Jesse Bright. Soon the two men had a political falling out. During the Bleeding Kansas era in the 1850s, in which a civil war was underway in Kansas, President Buchanan and his arch opponent Stephen Douglas battled each other over the Lecompton Kansas constitution—a pro slavery document. A Douglas ally reported from Washington, "The Lecompton constitution, so called, was prepared, word for word, in this city, under the especial supervision of.... Mr. Senator Bright."5

U.S Senator Jesse Bright (Library of Congress).

49

Senators Beholden to the People

Although Bright was a free state citizen he owned twenty-one slaves in Kentucky when the Civil War began. Ownership of slaves by citizens of free states and Territories was routine business. As long as these slaves were domiciled in free territory their owners retained full right to own them. In 1854 the *Chicago Daily Tribune* reported that Bright "pays for his 'brandy smashes'—no small number—... by selling off, occasionally, when he gets 'hard up,' a man, woman, or child, according to the extent of his necessities." Described as "a rough-and-tumble athlete and bully," he was found to be consulting with Jefferson Davis, apparently to supply Confederate forces with improvements in firearms technology:

> Washington, March 1, 1861
>
> MY DEAR SIR: Allow me to introduce to your acquaintance my friend Thomas B. Lincoln, of Texas. He visits your capital mainly to dispose of what he regards a great improvement in fire-arms. I recommend him to your favorable consideration as a gentleman of the first respectability, and reliable in every respect.
>
> Very truly, yours,
JESSE D. BRIGHT
>
> To His Excellency JEFFERSON DAVIS,
> *President of the Confederation of States.*

In a floor speech Sen. Timothy Howe declared, "The people of the United States ... have a right to be represented here by their friends, not by their enemies, by those who adhere to their Government, and not by those who would help overthrow it." Howe added, "The Constitution demands that every man who has a seat here, and undertakes to legislate for the people of the United States shall be a friend to them." In contrast Jesse Bright in July 1861 gave a speech declaring he was "not willing to vote either men or money to invade States that have formally declared themselves out of the Union." Howe declared, "The Senator from Indiana is not disposed to maintain this Constitution; that he does not stand here a friend to this form of government." Howe was more than a slavery opponent; he was an enthusiastic abolitionist promoting their wider social reform agenda. President Grant offered to appoint him Chief Justice of the U.S. Supreme Court. Bright claimed his contact with Jefferson

Part 2. Election of Senators by State Legislatures

Davis was being misunderstood, but a majority of fellow Senators found his behavior treasonous. On January 30, 1862, U.S. Sen. David Wilmot spoke forthrightly: "We have the letter before us. *It was written to a traitor, and for a traitor, and to further a treasonable end.* What more does my colleague want? The Senator on trial has given us no facts or mitigating circumstances whatever." The Senate expelled him on February 5, 1862. U.S. Sen. Howe explained, "The Constitution and its supremacy have been struck at by an open, an undisguised, and an armed foe." In debate about Bright, Howe said, "The proposition of which the Senator from Indiana declared himself ... was a proposition which called upon the President to surrender every post, every fort, every garrison." Authorities confiscated Bright's property but filed no criminal charges against him. He moved to Kentucky where he enjoyed a successful subsequent political career. He was one of several Senators whose Southern sympathies earned them expulsion for disloyalty.

James F. Simmons

Republican James F. Simmons (W–RI) was a Rhode Island industrialist when that state was a center of manufacturing. Simmons started as a textile manufacturer, establishing the mill cities of Upper and Lower Simmonsville. He entered the U.S. Senate in 1841. He served with distinction but in 1862 Secretary of War Edwin Stanton reported that Simmons had agreed to use his influence as a Senator to get

U.S. Senator James F. Simmons (photograph by Julian Vannerson, 1859, Library of Congress).

Senators Beholden to the People

a lucrative arms contract for Rhode Island manufacturer Casper D. Schubarth in return for a $50,000 payment to Simmons.

Schubarth was a Norwegian immigrant who became a Rhode Island gun manufacturer. He developed innovations in breech loading rifles, improvements that merited favorable mention from the journal *Scientific American*. The journal noted that the rifle could send a bullet "through 15 one-inch boards at a distance of one hundred yards." Schubarth bragged that his design was "effective and sure, and not liable to explode by accident, and capable of very rapid firing." He added, "Its construction is simple and economical, and it is durable and not liable to repair." In October 1861 he began marketing his design to the U.S. Army and Navy, who were potential prime customers as the Civil War began. The federal government ordered 50,000 of the weapons.

U.S. Sen. James F. Simmons was a Civil War arms contractor whose conduct excited suspicion among his Senate colleagues and the War Department. Here are views of the kind of rifles manufactured by Simmons and his subcontractors (New York Public Library).

Part 2. Election of Senators by State Legislatures

Although he had support from scientists and engineers, Schubarth knew that having a superior product did not assure marketing success. A major drawback was that he didn't own a gun factory. He approached two Rhode Island textile barons, the fabulously wealthy brothers Amos D. and James Y. Smith, the latter of whom would soon become Rhode Island's governor. They pledged to finance the project and supplied Schubarth with a letter of introduction to Rhode Island's Republican U.S. Senator James F. Simmons who, rather to Schubarth's advantage, was Chairman of the Senate Committee on patents and formerly headed the Senate Committee on Manufactures.

Looking over the materials, Simmons jovially remarked to Schubarth that the two brothers back in Rhode Island had enough money themselves to afford payment of the customary commission on such a transaction. This compensation was a problem. Although Schubarth was a solid businessman, he was an immigrant and unfamiliar with customary expectations of doing business at this level. He said, "I heard that it was generally understood that a commission was paid for obtaining contracts" and Simmons expected to share in the arrangement. In fact, he frankly told Schubarth of various deals he was brokering, saying, "I shall be a rich man." Schubarth agreed to pay Simmons a 5 percent kickback (one dollar for each rifle).

Because Shubarth did not have a firearms factory, he instead subcontracted to manufacturers who could assemble a portion of each gun, rather in the style that smaller companies would get pieces of massive contracts in World War II, say, temperature gauges that would be installed on bomber instrument panels.

Back in Rhode Island the two Smith brothers backed off from Schubarth. Also word was getting around that Simmons had strong-armed War Department employees to approve the Schubarth contract. Schubarth acquired new financial backers who wanted a firm commitment from Senator Simmons that he would get their share of the Schubarth contract firmed up. Arrangements were achieved that were satisfactory to all parties: Shubarth, his new backers, Senator Simmons, and the War Department. Until the new War Secretary arrived on the scene. Secretary Edwin Stanton replaced Cameron and began careful inspection of arms contracts; Schubarth's attracted his attention. In cooperation with the Senate, Stanton appointed a commission to ascertain the circumstances of Schubarth's professional relationship with Simmons. In addition Shubarth began asking Stanton for an extension of contractual deadlines so he would not go into default. "I am doing my best," Schubarth said. Stanton was not a good destination for such a request; historian Ida Tarbell was succinct: "He made open war on contractors." Stanton had little patience for either arms contractors or Congressional investigators. He acted as if members of Congress were part of the problem. Senator Powell indignantly informed his colleagues, "I called on the honorable Secretary of War this morning with a view to read the report [about Schubarth and Simmons]. He was guilty of the very great incivility of refusing me the privilege of reading the report in his office.... I wanted it for the purpose of aiding me in legislation.... I hope that now the Secretary will have the official starch knocked out of him, and not hereafter give such a reply to a Senator."[6] Investigators noted, "The committee would further state in this connection that it was the common practice until a recent period for members of Congress to prosecute claims against the Government for fees and rewards, and that for many years our most distinguished public men were in the habit of prosecuting claims under such circumstances without censure or criticism; but this was made a misdemeanor by an act of Congress in 1853, and since that period the practice has been discontinued."[7] Under the law of 1853 the influence pedaling of Simmons was illegal, but it was not illegal enough to deter Simmons's type of conduct, and a tougher law was enacted in 1862. In some circles regret was expressed that prosecuting Simmons under the new law would be an *ex post facto* proceeding forbidden by the Constitution.

On July 2 Sen. Joseph Wright (IN–R) submitted a resolution saying "it appears that the senator from the State of Rhode Island, James F. Simmons, gave and exercised his official influence over certain of the heads of the departments of our government in procuring for one C.D. Schubarth an order, dated October 11, 1861, authorizing the said Schubarth, in behalf of the government, to manufacture, for the use of the army and navy, fifty thousand breech-loading rifles; and, further, that the said senator did agree to receive, as a compensation for services rendered in such procurement, the sum of fifty thousand dollars.... Resolved, That the said James F. Simmons be, and is hereby, expelled from the seat he holds in this Senate."[8] Simmons resigned before his colleagues could expel him, returning to Rhode Island mercantile pursuits. Like the Senator, Schubarth went back to Rhode Island where he pursued business interests unrelated to arming Union forces.

Simon Cameron

Sen. Simon Cameron of Pennsylvania had assorted business interests which he continued to run while he was in the Senate. These ranged from insurance and banking to iron forging to newspaper editing and to developing dockyards, canals and railways. In the 1830s he also made money as a state commissioner in charge of dealing with Indian claims. One observer reported that "wholesale frauds were being perpetrated on the Indians," who had to accept payment for their claims in notes from a bank where Cameron was cashier. When he was first elected to the U.S. Senate one of his critics declared, "Simon Cameron's the Senator! God save the Commonwealth."[9] Cameron was President Lincoln's first Secretary of War. Described by President Polk as "a managing, tricky man in whom no reliance is to be placed,"[10] and by someone else as "a most valuable friend and a most dangerous enemy,"[11] Cameron had a reputation for shady dealings. Lincoln was looking for an administrator, not a saint, but Cameron's known conduct incensed many persons. Some Pennsylvanian legislators were after him when in 1857 when he appeared in Washington to be sworn in as Senator. His enemies told the Senate Judiciary Committee "that the election of the said Simon Cameron was procured ... by corrupt and unlawful means, influencing the action and votes of certain members of the house of representatives of this State [Pennsylvania]." The majority of the committee said the accusations were too vague to justify investigation and the committee's declaration ended the matter. That was not an exoneration, however. Indeed, the committee minority argued that "the accusation comes from a responsible source, and is too serious, too distinctly and directly made, to be treated with indifference." The Senators who investigated may have

Simon Cameron was a prominent Pennsylvania businessman, treated with suspicion by those who dealt with him. President Polk described him as a "managing tricky man in whom no reliance can be placed." Many persons considered him corrupt, but he did have ideals. For example, in 1858 he declared: "There never has been a time ... when there was so much real distress among the laboring men of my State—the men who do the work, the men who go to the forge before daylight, and remain there long after the moon has risen.... The time is coming when they will control the politics of this country." Also, after a Southern member of Congress beat up U.S. Senator Charles Sumner of Massachusetts, Cameron and several other Northern Senators pledged to prevent a repeat attack or die trying (Library of Congress).

forgotten about it soon enough, but the public had a long memory for allegations of corruption. So did Lincoln whose private files contained many reports about Cameron's conduct. Lincoln's biographer (and Progressive Republican) Ida Tarbell later wrote that under Cameron "contracts were awarded for politics' sake and that the government was being swindled wholesale."[12]

> "We hear," said the "Evening Post" in June [1861], "of knapsacks glued together and falling to pieces after the first day's use; of uniform coats which are torn to pieces with a slight pull of the fingers; of blankets too small if they were good, and too poor stuff to be useful if they were of the proper size, shoes, caps, trousers, coats—all too often of such poor material that before a soldier is ready for service he must be clothed anew."

Tarbell noted, "The matter was too serious a one for Mr. Lincoln to overlook. The public would not have permitted him to overlook it."[13]

Many persons considered Cameron corrupt, but he did have ideals. For example, in 1858 he declared: "There never has been a time ... when there was so much real distress among the laboring men of my State—the men who do the work, the men who go to the forge before daylight, and remain there long after the moon has risen.... The time is coming when they will control the politics of this country." Also, after a Southern member of Congress beat up U.S. Senator Charles Sumner of Massachusetts, Cameron and several other Northern Senators pledged to prevent a repeat attack or die trying.

Samuel Pomeroy

During the 1850s in Kansas, Samuel Pomeroy helped found the town of Lawrence, which attracted hostile attention from slavery proponents. For his willingness to put his body on the line for freedom he earned a lot of credit from opponents of slavery. In 1873, however, he was accused of bribing Kansas legislators to win election to the U.S. Senate in the previous year. Samuel Pomeroy's name was frequently connected with rumors of corruption and bribery during his political career in Kansas. He has been described as one who "weighed everything by a money standard. He has judged all public measures by the cash that was in them; and estimated all men by the amount it would take to buy them."¹⁴ His Senate colleague Edmund Ross (R–KS) noted that Pomeroy acquired tens of thousands of acres from Indian tribes and "he stole from the Central Branch Railroad company, consisting of government and railroad mortgage bonds given to it as a subsidy."¹⁵ Describing to a business partner a convoluted way through which they could profit from the Indian trade, Pomeroy concluded, "We have nothing to do, only to take our share profits at each payment."¹⁶ As such conduct became public, one newspaper headline proclaimed, "The modus operandi of a Senatorial Indian Steal—How some Senators are made Millionaires on Senatorial Salaries of $5,000 a year."¹⁷

U.S Sen. Samuel Pomeroy of Kansas (Library of Congress).

One newspaper described Pomeroy's conduct as follows: "Pomeroy entered upon the [1872] Senatorial contest with all the careful and elaborate preparations of an experienced general." Long before the fall election he had sent out his mandate to his postmasters and office holders: "Fix things at your end of the line, and I will fix things here."¹⁸ Pomeroy funded state legislature candidates in every county and ran his own candidates where county officials opposed him.

Newspapers were edited by his political henchmen. The *Lawrence Tribune* was owned by Postmaster Shimmons. The *Atchison Champion* was owned by Postmaster Martin. The *Paola Spirit* was owned by Postmaster Perry. The *Parsons Sun* was owned by U.S. Land Office

Part 2. Election of Senators by State Legislatures

Receiver Reynolds. *The Commonwealth* was owned by Adams & Veal and other Topeka speculators who wanted contracts for State printing. Railroads gave tangible support in the guise of passes entitling his supporters to free transportation.

U.S. Senate investigators concluded that his conduct was acceptable, but in 1873 another investigation was held due to a speech that state senator Alexander York made in January before the state legislature started voting. He

> stated that on Monday night he had visited Senator Pomeroy's room, in the dark and secret recesses of the Tefft House, and there, in an interview with the Senator, bargained his vote for the said Pomeroy, in consideration of $8,000.... In corroboration of the astounding disclosure, Col. York advanced to the Chief Clerk's desk, and placed upon it two parcels of money, which he desired should be counted and held thereafter for the expenses of prosecuting S.C. Pomeroy for bribery and corruption. The packages were found to contain, one $2,000 and the other $5,000–$7,000 in all.[19]

In that speech York gave details about a $7,000 bribe that Pomeroy had paid to him for his promised vote, with another $1,000 to come after York actually gave his vote.

The legislature proceeded to elect a U.S. Senator. Pomeroy received no votes. The winner by a landslide was John Ingalls.

The Kansas legislature appointed a committee to investigate Pomeroy, which found that Pomeroy had also used an agent to bribe another legislator. Pomeroy claimed the cash was intended to help set up a bank but acknowledged that no receipt was given or taken for the thousands of dollars in cash. U.S. Senate investigators made their report on the last day of Pomeroy's term, concluding that the case against Pomeroy was unproven. No further proceedings were held.

John Ingalls

When Republican U.S. Senator John Ingalls (no relation to the novelist) ran for reelection in 1879 he left the state to return to Washington, D.C. For a candidate to absent himself at the climax of an election campaign is never a good idea, but Ingalls probably felt his effort among state legislators in Topeka was in competent hands. Although Ingalls prevailed in the balloting, his margin of victory was narrow.

A number of his opponents then contacted the U.S. Senate and claimed election irregularities. An investigation by the Kansas legislature concluded that Ingalls benefited from bribery and other corruption. The U.S. Senate decided to scrutinize the situation and conducted hearings in Topeka and Washington, producing a report of more than 500 pages. In the 1800s, Kansas politics was a rugged occupation. Senate investigators got an earful of stories about secret meetings of inebriated state legislators: "Did Mr. Merritt tell you at that time that you were a damned blackmailing scoundrel ... and that he ought to put you out of the window?" Investigators concluded that "bribery and other corrupt means were employed" to promote the candidacy of Ingalls. The U.S. Senate decided, however, that proof of participation by Ingalls in illegalities was lacking and, moreover, the admitted irregularities of him and his supporters had not affected the election's outcome. Senate investigation of the matter ceased.[20]

U.S. Senator John J. Ingalls (Library of Congress).

The committee's majority reported[21] that "bribery and other corrupt means were employed by persons favoring the election of Hon. John J. Ingalls." "Other means" included failure to obey subpoenas ("E.L. Smith, general manager of the Western Union Telegraph Co.,

Part 2. Election of Senators by State Legislatures

Topeka ... refused to testify and also refused to produce a large number of important telegrams sent ... by Mr. Ingalls and his agents"). Kansas state legislators who would be voting on whether to reelect Ingalls had reports such as these: "I was personally approached by John J. Ingalls for my vote, and was offered money provided I would vote for him. The sum agreed upon was one thousand dollars." "J.B. Clogston ... was approached personally by Mr. Ingalls ... [and] was offered by said agents five hundred dollars to vote for Mr. Ingalls." "A member of the [Kansas statehouse], was offered three hundred dollars by one person and eight hundred dollars by another to vote for Mr. Ingalls, and that said persons offering the bribes were agents of Mr. Ingalls." A house member "was paid two hundred and fifty dollars to vote for Mr. Ingalls, and ... said money was paid by an agent of Mr. Ingalls." Another house member "was offered the sum of five hundred dollars to vote for Mr. Ingalls, and ... the person offering the bribe was an agent of Mr. Ingalls." A similar list of other legislators existed which named the persons involved.

Ingalls offered to appoint someone postmaster at the town of Atchison in return for a vote for Ingalls in the state legislature. "Another" said he "was an Ingalls man ... and he said that if Mr. Ingalls was elected he would get a beef contract to furnish beef for an Indian territory." A cooperative federal marshal obtained names of grand jury members to discourage them from returning indictments. Legislators were known to change allegiance in order to support Ingalls. One legislator "stated that he had been offered a thousand dollars for his vote, and that they had paid him $200 of the money and were to pay the balance of five hundred before the election and five hundred afterwards.... He said that he had a personal interview with Mr. Ingalls. The legislator stated that he had told Mr. Ingalls he was poor and that his vote was a matter of business with him."

J.A. Hossack stated, "As a member of the legislature.... I was approached personally by John J. Ingalls for my vote, and was offered money provided I would vote for him. The sum agreed upon was one thousand dollars." Favors discussed included Ingalls helping to pay debts of legislators who would help him.

Senators Beholden to the People

Senator Bailey asked, "Is Mr. Shaw accessible?" Mr. Peck replied, "We have been informed that he cannot be found. I am informed that a praecipe was filed for him and a telegram sent, to which the operator replied that he had left town."

The committee's minority reported: "We exonerate Mr. Ingalls from complicity with improper practices." The state of Kansas donated a statue of Ingalls which was displayed in the U.S. Capitol's Statuary Hall. Ingalls later stated to reformers who might be disturbed by his election, "The Decalogue and the Golden Rule have no place in a political campaign." He added, "The purification of politics ... is an iridescent dream. Government is force. Politics is a battle for supremacy.... The object is success."

Stephen W. Dorsey

Around 1881 investigators put the conduct of Sen. Stephen W. Dorsey (R–AR) under a magnifying glass while looking into the so-called Star Route Post Office scandal. He and associates were accused of lightening the public purse by several million dollars. Dorsey was indicted for fraud, but although he was found not guilty, his finances and reputation were ruined.

After the Civil War, Ohio native Dorsey became a member of the city council in Sandusky, Ohio, where he ran a mercantile business, traded in cotton, made barrels, and got gas illumination in town.

U.S. Senator Stephen W. Dorsey (Library of Congress).

Part 2. Election of Senators by State Legislatures

With the start of 1870, Dorsey resigned his seat on the city council, collected letters of introduction from influential Ohioans, including Governor Hayes, and prepared to move his residence to Arkansas as a carpetbagger.

There he became president of the Arkansas Central Railway, along with several others. His industrious work as a railroad builder generated support in the state legislature for electing him to the U.S. Senate despite, or because of, his status as a carpetbagger which gave him connections in the national Republican scene. Declared the Democratic *Helena World* about Dorsey: "Though a Republican of the strictest school, [he] is not devoid of principle [and], our people have found him to be a good citizen in every respect." The *Gazette* said, "If he has stolen anything, stuffed any ballot-boxes, or been a party to any such conduct, or in any manner aided or abetted in oppressing the people, we have not heard of it."

In January 1873 the Arkansas legislature elected Dorsey to the

An 1884 *Puck* magazine cartoon shows the Republican Party trying to carry its leaders. It depicts Stephen W. Dorsey and Thomas J. Brady in sacks labeled "Star Route Swindle" (Library of Congress).

Senators Beholden to the People

U.S. Senate. The *Helena World* newspaper commented, "The labor and means expended on the Central [Railway] have made [Dorsey], according to report, a man of wealth, enabling him to spend, to secure his election to the United States Senate, some sixty or seventy thousand dollars." That expenditure is an example of the huge valuation put on a U.S. Senate seat. The *Arkadelphia Standard* described Dorsey as "a man of fair ability, indifferently honest as the times go, having never been caught stealing anything bigger than a railroad."

In the nation's capital Dorsey was not diligent in attending floor votes but did engage in committee work. His appointment to the District of Columbia Committee had initially placed him under suspicion of collusion with boss Alexander Shepherd and the "D.C. Ring" of street paving contractors. Although examination of the "Ring" in 1874 failed to implicate Dorsey, his reputation remained suspect, and in 1877 he was openly accused of using his position on the District of Columbia Committee to benefit himself. In March 1877, newspaper reports appeared that Dorsey was stopping action on a bill affecting the District's

Evidence spraying Dorsey (*Puck*, March 7, 1883, Library of Congress).

Part 2. Election of Senators by State Legislatures

creditors, pending payment to him of $25,000. Dorsey never shook the reputation that his vote was for sale.

In the spring of 1878 news media fingered Dorsey for alleged irregularities connected with granting Post Office Department contracts for carrying the mail. Dorsey had supposedly sent mail contract bids to a postmaster friend in direct violation of postal regulations. A further claim was that after these bids were signed and returned to Dorsey in Washington, someone added the names of his brother John and brother-in-law John Peck.

Congress conducted an investigation into the postal contracts awarded to Dorsey's friends and into Dorsey's own connection to mail contracts. This inquiry failed to show that Dorsey had done anything illegal concerning mail contracts or that anything criminal had occurred at all. Indeed, evidence presented to the committee showed that Senator Dorsey simply did for his personal friends what was ordinary for members of Congress to do. But a charge that Dorsey belonged to a corrupt Post Office Ring, stealing millions from the treasury annually, resurfaced as part of an effort to discredit him.

After inconclusive findings in 1878, Congress had conducted a second examination of postal contract irregularities, concentrating on Second Assistant Postmaster General Thomas J. Brady, and investigators focused entirely on the workings of Brady's office.

Barely a month into President Garfield's term huge frauds were uncovered in the Post Office Department, for which Dorsey, his brother, and brother-in-law were prosecuted. Dorsey was acquitted in two trials. So-called Star Routes paid extra money to private carriers of mail. Often this additional income was due to "expedition services" by which mail received expedited service. Dorsey made arrangements with dozens of subcontractors to "share the wealth." He had 134 Star Routes, which had become known as the "Dorsey combination." A falling out occurred among the many associates. This situation became tense when President Garfield ordered the Attorney General to make a full investigation of the Post Office situation. Since in the 1880 presidential election Dorsey had been charge of the Republican National Committee and manager of Garfield's campaign, the newly elected

Senators Beholden to the People

President could not afford to disregard the situation. The Postmaster of New York City told Dorsey to his face that his Star Route manipulations were illegal.

The so-called Star Route Post Office frauds were one of the great scandals of the Gilded Age and were attributed to Sen. Stephen Dorsey. Despite two acquittals Dorsey realized that his reputation and fortune were ruined. Dorsey's reputation never recovered from treatment he received from Star Route prosecutors. He relocated from Arkansas to New Mexico Territory where, along with New Mexico business partners such as Gilded Age politicians James G. Blaine and Stephen B. Elkins, Dorsey speculated in land, cattle, mining, and a number of other enterprises.

Henry B. Payne

In 1884 Ohio Democratic legislators caucused to pick a U.S. Senator. George Pendleton, the 1864 Democratic candidate for Vice President and notable for his opposition to the Thirteenth Amendment, sought the Ohio senatorial selection in 1884, as did Durbin Ward. These two were the only candidates mentioned when the October state legislature election leading to the U.S. Senate balloting by the state legislature was held. A third candidate suddenly appeared, Democrat Henry B. Payne. "With but little premonition, so far as observed by the public, his

Many persons believed Henry B. Payne's election to the U.S. Senate was due to influence from the Standard Oil Company (Library of Congress).

Part 2. Election of Senators by State Legislatures

candidacy came upon the party with a force and character that challenged the ability of the friends of the other candidates to withstand. There seemed to be something in its character calculated to overawe them, and to crush opposition...." The Ohio house of representatives established an investigating committee, which reported, "Messengers were found to be traversing the State in the interest of the candidacy of Mr. Payne." The committee report went on:

> Newspapers suddenly changed position in his favor, and avowed friends of the other candidates were found to be wavering or to have deserted.... In the general stampede that was being made here, and the pressure that was brought to bear, a man could hardly rely upon himself. It took continued prompting to have me feel that I was not a Payne man myself.... The Standard Oil Company, with its officers and workers, were here in force. The Secretary and the Treasurer of the company were here, and there was the unlimited use of money to bring the friends of every member of the Legislature here from their own counties, for the purpose of laboring with them to support Mr. Payne.

The committee report further stated:

> Bribery is not easily proven. Our laws make the giver and taker of a bribe equally guilty, and visit both with the same penalty, which is doubtless just, but the effect of which is to bind the guilty parties together in a bond of secrecy that neither can break without imperiling his own liberty. When the crime has been determined upon and committed deliberately, the parties thereto will adopt every means to conceal it—not only such ingenuity as is exercised by criminals in the preparation and commission of crime, but perjury as well to prevent its discovery; so that it is only by circumstantial evidence—by unguarded and unintentional admissions, or by the sudden and undue acquisition of property, and other significant circumstances, and rarely by direct evidence, that the charge can be sustained.

The committee summarized:

> There is a general concurrence of testimony upon the following points:
>
> 1. That the candidacy of Henry B. Payne for United States Senator was not made known publicly until a considerable time after the general election of 1883, at which members of the General Assembly were chosen.
>
> 2. That suspicion and charges of the employment of illegal means to secure the election of the successful candidate for Senator were very

Senators Beholden to the People

prevalent near the time of, and for weeks after, the Senatorial election, and that in many instances the suspicion amounted almost to conviction.

3. That as to choice of Senatorial candidates among members of the General Assembly, there were numerous remarkable changes, difficult to account for without assuming the use of unusual inducements.

Payne received a comfortable majority of ballots, but his opponents noted that his son Oliver had said Henry Payne's election had cost Oliver $100,000. That amount may have impressed Ohio legislators but was simply chump change for Oliver, who died with an estate worth $32 million. He made that money not only from Standard Oil but also from organizing American Tobacco and U.S. Steel. Too, Henry's opponents argued that if caucus members had been forced to give public votes to Payne instead of secret ballots, influence by Standard might have been plainer. Suspicion of corruption arose.

An investigator[22] noted that one David R. Paige was recognized as a confidential manager for the successful candidate for Senator. "A [businessman] ... had just that day come down from Akron had gone into a small tailor shop.... A young man burst into the store, and, in an excited manner, ran to

Standard was targeted by a nursery rhyme in *Puck*, 1904 (Library of Congress).

Part 2. Election of Senators by State Legislatures

Standard Oil was portrayed as a lawless octopus squeezing the republic (Library of Congress, ca. 1901).

the proprietor of the store, and said he had ... never seen so much money together as he saw in an inner room attached to the room occupied by Mr. Payne as headquarters...."

J.J. Hall, of Akron, testified:

> I had a conversation with Mr. Mueller—ex-Lieutenant-Governor Mueller.... He went into Mr. Paige's room. He said it looked to him like a banking-house. There was a large amount of money in plain view.... Excitement was very high, ... and I was witnessing the process that was going on between the Payne headquarters ... and Dave Paige's room. There were canvass bags, and coin bags, and cases for greenbacks littered and scattered around the room, and on the table, and on the floor, and he said by his foot was one of the bags lying with something green sticking out from the end of it, ... and he kicked the bag off from it, and he saw it lying there all crumpled up, and just out of idle curiosity, more than anything else, he picked it up and found it to be a twenty or a ten dollar greenback—I don't know which now—and he showed it to this man that was sitting there... and the man said: "That's all right—keep it."

"The stuff was being used there to buy votes for Mr. Payne."

The investigating committee tracked examples.

"Case of Ex-Representative Kahle. Mr. Kahle testified that O.B. Ramey, the senator from his district, offered him five thousand dollars to vote for Payne for Senator, and that he made this proposition to him on two occasions, on one of which he said that he would stick the money in one of witness's pockets."

"Case of Representative Hull. Mr. Hull, a member of the last and also of the present House, testified that Hon. Charles Negley said to him, two or three days prior to the Senatorial caucus, that he (Negley) believed the witness could get twenty-five hundred dollars to vote against Pendleton and for Payne."

"L. A. Russell, of Cleveland, testified that, on the night of the Senatorial caucus, and just before the caucus assembled, in the hall of the Neil House in front of the Pendleton and Ward headquarters, Mr. Hull came up to him, manifesting very considerable symptoms of excitement, and said: 'Mr. Russell, a man just offered me twenty-five hundred dollars in currency, in an open envelope, to vote for Payne, and by G—d I am going over to that caucus, and I am going to get up in the caucus and name the man and denounce him.'"

"Rumors as to suspected bribery, with which were connected the names of Messrs. Mooney and Roche, members of the House, and Messrs. White and Ramey, members of the Senate, of the Sixty-sixth General Assembly, all of whom voted in caucus for Henry B. Payne for United States Senator, were traced by the committee."

Calls grew for the Senate to expel Payne, but he kept his seat. Later scholarship concluded that a good circumstantial case could be made that corruption occurred in Payne's election.[23]

Charles Henry Dietrich

Nebraska governor Charles Henry Dietrich became a U.S. Senator in 1901. He took a bribe to get Jacob Fisher appointed as a U.S. postmaster and to get the federal government to rent a building.[24]

On February 1, 1904, Dietrich said,

"Mr. President, I rise to a question of personal privilege. By a Federal grand jury at Omaha I have recently been indicted for alleged violation

Part 2. Election of Senators by State Legislatures

of the laws of the United States, and on a trial of the indictments before a Federal court at Omaha was discharged by the Federal judge without the cause being heard upon its merits, upon the ground that my acts were no violation of the Federal law. Before taking further part in the deliberations of this body I owe a duty to the Senate, whose honor has been assailed, to the State which in part I represent, whose credit has been attacked, and to myself, whose integrity has been impugned. If guilty of the least of these charges, I deserve to be driven from this high place in disgrace and receive the severest penalty of the criminal law. Confident in my innocence, I desire to submit the whole matter to the Senate." Thereupon Mr. Dietrich submitted a resolution, which was agreed to, as follows: "Resolved, That the President pro tempore shall appoint a committee of five to investigate and report to the Senate all the facts."

In 1904 proceedings against Dietrich were abandoned on grounds that the offense occurred before Dietrich took his senatorial oath of office. A U.S. Senate investigation concluded that Dietrich had not engaged in wrongful conduct. Still, the behavior of Dietrich and Fisher fitted that of bribery regardless of whether the U.S. Senate was in session at the time. Plus, the wording of the federal indictment, though it may have been standard boilerplate language, did not inspire public confidence in Dietrich: "Charles H. Dietrich, and he, the said Jacob Fisher, did then and there unlawfully, corruptly, and wickedly conspire, combine, confederate, and agree together and with each other to commit an offense against the United States and to violate a law of the United States, to wit, section one thousand seven hundred and eighty-one of the Revised Statutes of the United States, by the said Charles H. Dietrich then and there fraudulently, willfully, corruptly, unlawfully, and knowingly agreeing with the said Joseph Fisher to take and receive the sum of one thousand three hundred dollars from the said Jacob Fisher."

Dietrich remained a Senator until 1905.

Isaac Stephenson

The Wisconsin general assembly chose lumber magnate Isaac Stephenson as a U.S. Senator in 1907. Given that he was a forthright supporter of the Progressive Republican agenda, there is irony in charges laid against him for bribery and corruption. These accusations

Senators Beholden to the People

came two years after Stephenson took his seat, so there was a question of timeliness in the complaint. Wisconsin was a state that used a "direct primary" in choosing U.S. Senators. Under this method, in state elections voters could name their choice for U.S. Senator. This was a work-around for getting U.S. Senators elected by voters without adopting the Seventeenth Amendment. This ballot box expression of popularity had no official role in the process of electing a Senator, but often state legislators were influenced strongly enough by this expression of voter preference that the winner of the "direct primary" would be elected as a U.S. Senator by the state legislature. Indeed, support for this "direct primary" method of choosing a U.S. Senator grew so strong that it became one of the last topics on which members of a state legislature were instructed. In 1910 the Oregon general assembly proclaimed one of the last instructions from a state legislature to a congressional delegation: "We, the people of the State of Oregon, hereby instruct our representatives and senators in our legislative assembly, as such officers, to vote for and elect the candidates for U.S. Senators from this State who receive the highest number of votes at our general elections."[25]

A good showing in the primary balloting was thus important, and Stephenson spent more than $107,000 for the 1908 direct primary. Indeed, Senate investigators found his expenditure to be closer to $250,000. Stephenson spent so much on his primary election that his campaign was described as de facto bribery of voters. A Senate subcommittee traveled from Washington to Wisconsin to hear about the situation firsthand. His supporters expressed indifference about generating records and even about retaining records. In postage alone the Stephenson campaign spent $12,000. He rented a headquarters in a hotel. He hired seventy workers to distribute cash and personally handed $2,500 to a game warden. Fifteen months into his term the U.S Senate received a memorial from the Wisconsin legislature charging him with getting elected through bribing state legislators. A Senate inquiry absolved him of that charge, although he acknowledged supplying cash to be used for his benefit by state legislators. He also paid persons to collect signatures on nominating petitions. He hired speakers, halls, bands, and "get out the vote" staff along with passing around drinks and cigars. A minority report from the Senate Privileges and Elections committee declared that "the methods employed at the primary were corrupt; that they were against public policy; stated that they were demoralizing in character; that they directly contributed to destroy the purity and freedom of the election; that they violated the fundamental principles at the basis of our system of government; and that they are not to be tolerated by the Senate of the United States as a means of procuring a seat in that body."

Fortunately for Stephenson, although several aspects of his conduct had become illegal subsequent to his campaign activity, they were legal at the time he was doing them, and like any person, he was immune from ex post facto proceedings. His conduct was so extravagant that it created indignation among some Wisconsin residents, but they gave him a pass due to his advanced age and his long-standing support of Republican principles (he had joined the Republican Party in 1854 when the Kansas-Nebraska Act was a live issue, and in 1911 he was helping the Party's Progressive wing headed by Theodore Roosevelt). Stephenson held on to his Senate seat by a margin of two votes from his colleagues.

William A. Clark

When the Civil War began William A. Clark purportedly fought for the Confederacy. He soon deserted and headed for Western mine country in Colorado and Montana. There he established a company store selling supplies at inflated prices, finding that outfitting prospectors was far more lucrative than prospecting itself. Afterward he moved from supplies into smelting and milling where he made a fortune and became known as one of Montana's three "copper kings," the others being F. Augustus Heinze and Marcus Daly.

In 1899 he ran as a Democrat for the U.S. Senate, faced by Republican Marcus Daly. Each man was wealthy, and in the election contest they spent freely of their private fortunes, purchasing newspaper editors and fellow politicians. Clark reputedly spent more than

Senators Beholden to the People

$300,000 in bribing the Montana state legislature to elect him. One legislator displayed $30,000 in cash that he claimed Clark was paying for his vote. Investigators found that Clark's son was supervising the bribery operation. The bribery campaign was not always overt; a recipient might have a mortgage paid or sell a parcel of real estate for an inflated price. Clark thereby began his U.S. Senate service under a cloud, accused of bribing the state legislature that chose him. At first he was allowed to take his seat in Washington, but a Senate committee unanimously recommended that he be expelled by the Senate because of the bribery scheme, and Clark thereupon returned to Montana where, supposedly under the influence of bribes, the general assembly elected him again. In responding to criticism of his buying the Montana legislature, Clark is reported to have said, "I never bought a man who wasn't for sale."

Newspaper cartoons publicized reports that William A. Clark bribed his way into the U.S. Senate (Library of Congress).

He entered the Senate a second time in 1901. This time he served a full term until 1907 despite accusations that he once again was bribing legislators to get their votes. During his campaign he promised miners an eight-hour workday, but he reneged after he was elected. Mark Twain expressed his view of Clark: "He is as rotten a human being as can be found anywhere under the flag; he is a shame to the American

Part 2. Election of Senators by State Legislatures

nation, and no one has helped to send him to the Senate who did not know that his proper place was the penitentiary, with a ball and chain on his legs. To my mind he is the most disgusting creature that the republic has produced since Tweed's time."[26] Clark was not known for industriousness in Washington. Fellow Senators said of him, "If you took away the whiskers and the scandal there would be nothing left."

After Clark retired from the senatorship in 1907 he moved to New York City where he became a banker living in a 100-room Fifth Avenue mansion on "Millionaires Row" across the street from

A political cartoon from *The Anaconda Standard* (Montana), October 28, 1900. Note the servant carrying a money bag from which Clark dipped cash to toss through a window transom (Wikipedia).

Central Park. He owned assorted corporations such as a newspaper, a wholesale operation, a wire plant, a blasting powder company, a mail delivery contract, a logging operation, and a beet sugar plantation. He was also involved in retail merchandising.

Like Sen. John Hipple Mitchell, Clark had a romantic life that attracted public attention. Clark was estranged from his family; his wife and children lived in Europe. Clark had a long-standing affair with Anna Eugenia La Chapelle, who he met when she was no more than sixteen years old. He sponsored music lessons for her in France and became notorious for seducing young women.

After serving one term, Clark retired from the Senate.

Joseph R. Burton

Crooked dealings by U.S. Senators became notorious. For example, saying he had suffered heavy losses in a financial panic, around 1903 Sen. Joseph R. Burton (R–KS) was looking for a way to recoup. He decided to charge fees for representing Rialto Grain and Securities Company in fraud proceedings that the U.S. Post Office was conducting against the corporation, which engaged in nationwide solicitation of investors by mail. "The Senator said to me, 'Cochran, I want to continue to appear before the [Post Office] Department in this and other cases, because I can make

Joseph Burton (Wikipedia).

Part 2. Election of Senators by State Legislatures

some money in that way to apply on my old debts.' He said had lost very heavily in the panic, and that he had paid about seventy thousand dollars of debts.... He said there wasn't anything wrong in this; that a number of Senators—Senator [George] Edmunds among them—had materially increased their income in this way, and that it was entirely proper."[27] Upon agreeing on a monthly fee of $500, a Rialto official "told Senator Burton ... it would be his duty to cultivate the acquaintance of financiers, particularly people connected with Trust Companies and financial institutions."[28]

Burton remarked, "I am not going to do anything inconsistent with my duty as a Senator." Though he described this arrangement as legitimate and used by many of his Senate colleagues to make money on the side, Burton's approach had several drawbacks. One was the shady nature Rialto's operation. It targeted unsophisticated investors by mail with appeals such as these: "The time is ripe for shrewd manipulations." "We have made enormous profits for our customers.... Buy now while the price is extremely low, and your profits will be all the greater." "The Chicago Board of Trade, and the New York Stock and Cotton Exchange have presented opportunities within the past year from which, on small beginnings, great fortunes have been made." "Fortunes are made between dawn and dark by those who know and—act quickly." Supposedly Rialto was a grain dealer specializing in corn.

Contrary to Rialto's contractual agreement, it failed to return investors' money on demand. And Burton told a Rialto colleague to destroy letters Burton had written. "I think," the Senator said, "it is just as well not to have these things in existence," which probably made a bad impression on the jury that in 1904 found him guilty of violating § 1782 Rev.Stat., resulting in a six-month prison sojourn, a $2,500 fine, and disqualification from holding any federal office of honor, profit, or trust. Despite two hearings from the U.S. Supreme Court, Burton's conviction stood. He resigned from the Senate in June 1906.[29]

The next year Sen. John H. Mitchell (R–OR) was convicted of violating the same law that Burton had violated, § 1782 Rev.Stat.

Senators Beholden to the People

John Hipple Mitchell

Sen. John Hipple Mitchell (R–OR) helped implement several land swindles involving railroads while serving intermittently in the Senate for fifteen years as the nineteenth century ended. Warning signs existed that Mitchell's tenure would be troubled. He was a popular lawyer in Portland, Oregon, but he felt a need to go by several names: John Hipple Mitchell, John Mitchell Hipple, John H. Mitchell, and J.H. Mitchell. Confusing, but confusion is often the purpose when someone uses several names.

Some persons suspected that such caution was related to his impregnating a fifteen-year-old student when he was her twenty-six year-old teacher in Pennsylvania. Her father insisted on a shotgun wedding, to which Mitchell agreed when cornered. His young wife said the marriage failed because of his unfaithfulness, which included bringing "wanton women" into their house. Supposedly he said he would murder her if she ever revealed what was going on.

U.S. Senator John Hipple Mitchell (Library of Congress).

He moved to California with a mistress and deserted her. He then married a woman in Oregon City without divorcing his Pennsylvania spouse and carried on an affair with his new wife's sister.

Political opponents thoroughly vetted his private life, but Senate colleagues did not feel that his conduct merited expulsion from

Part 2. Election of Senators by State Legislatures

the Senate. His decision to use his influence to promote crooked land claims involving railroads and timber companies, however, proved to be his undoing. *Looters of the Public Domain*, a memoir written by a participant nicknamed "King of the Oregon Land Fraud Ring," recalled a scene: "Pulling two $1,000 bills out of my pocket, I placed them on the table in front of the Senator, with the remark that I considered his services well worth that amount."[30] Unsurprisingly, Mitchell opposed the Progressive reform movement.

Clarence Watson

The fabulously wealthy Clarence Watson was one of the last persons elected to the Senate by a state legislature (West Virginia's), entering the Senate in February 1911, where he had one of the worst attendance records for roll call votes. Upon his selection as Senator, Republicans in the general assembly accused him of winning election through bribery and called for an investigation. A bit more than a year after Watson took office, the state's Republican governor William Glasscock alleged that Watson had won the Senate election through bribery by railway interests and Standard Oil. On its face the accusation had thin evidence—the word of one West Virginia legislator who retracted the claim. A Senate investigating committee concluded that the allegation was baseless. Simultaneously with the Watson inquiry Sen.

U.S. Senator Clarence Wayland Watson (Wikipedia).

Senators Beholden to the People

William Chilton (D–WV) faced the same sort of charges from Glasscock and was exonerated by the Senate.[31]

William Lorimer

Sen. William Lorimer (R–IL) of Chicago was expelled from the U.S. Senate in 1912 for accepting bribes. "Chicago," one muckraker eulogized. "First in violence, deepest in dirt; loud, lawless, unlovely, ill-smelling, irreverent, new; an overgrown gawk of a village, the 'tough' among cities, a spectacle for the nation."[32]

Lorimer was elected to several terms in the U.S. House of Representatives at the start of the twentieth century. Noted for entertaining constituents with movies, concerts, and circuses, Lorimer wanted to step up to the U.S. Senate. But he ran into one of the classic problems encountered when state legislatures balloted for Senate candidates—a deadlock. Although he was a Republican he eventually convinced enough Democrats to support him to let him win and take a Senate seat in 1909.

For a year his term went along smoothly, but then the *Chicago Tribune* published an expose accusing Lorimer of obtaining his Senate position through bribery. When the U.S. Senate investigated the accusations, and a majority of Senators concluded that Lorimer was blameless, the politician and Lincoln scholar Albert Beveridge

William Lorimer (Library of Congress). [MOU1]

Part 2. Election of Senators by State Legislatures

(R–IN) strongly dissented, arguing that the testimony of state legislators who admitted they accepted or paid bribes on Lorimer's behalf was credible. Beveridge was particularly struck that the alleged bribery would have nudged Lorimer into victory by one vote. Beveridge was also intrigued that the legislators in question possessed large denominations of cash right after the transaction supposedly happened. Beveridge was skeptical that Lorimer would have failed to attend to the alleged bribery with the same meticulous attention he gave to all other aspects of his campaigns. Progressives supporting passage of the Seventeenth Amendment argued that it would stop the bribing of state legislators to get their votes for Senator, and Beveridge received enthusiastic support in Progressive circles. At a dinner, Progressive Republican leader Theodore Roosevelt declined to sit at the same table with Lorimer.

Sen. Robert LaFollette (R–WI) then got involved, noting news media reports that business executives had created a $100,000 fund to bribe state legislators voting on whether Lorimer should be elected to the U.S. Senate.

The Progressive Republican magazine *The Voter* devoted considerable coverage to Lorimer's corrupt dealings, presenting a case study of what Progressives hoped to banish from public life via the Seventeenth Amendment. In covering the Lorimor case *The Voter* portrayed disputes among millionaires and spoke of "ironies of fate such as Balzac loved to develop in the Comedie Humaine." The magazine reported

> the Helm investigating committee at [the state capital of] Springfield dug up evidence that reopens the whole case. Trails leading in the direction of the men higher up "were at last discovered; evidence of a $100,000 corruption fund for use in the Lorimer election revealed...." H.H. Kohlsaat, editor of the *Chicago Record-Herald*, was the agency through which the crater was blown off the supposedly extinct volcano.... Mr. Kohlsaat's informant offered to go before the investigators as a witness. This man is Clarence S. Funk, general manager of the International Harvester Company. Mr. Funk's responsibility may be seen from the fact that he is in active control of 97,000 employees scattered over all quarters of the globe. His testimony gave the committee the first lead in the direction of the "men higher up" that has been found....

Senators Beholden to the People

Mr. Funk testified that shortly after the election of Senator Lorimer he was approached in the Union League Club, Chicago, by millionaire lumberman Edward Hines. "He said I was just the fellow he had been looking for or trying to see," said Funk, "and he said he wanted to talk to me a minute." We went away and sat down in one of the leather couches at the side of the room. Without any preliminaries, and quite as matter of course, he said: "Well, we put Lorimer over."

Hines asked Funk to contribute $10,000 as his assessment towards a $100,000 corruption fund which had been raised for Lorimer. Mr. Funk repulsed Hines with scorn. During the conversation, Funk said that Hines told him to send the money to Ed Tilden. Mr. Tilden is president of the National Packing Company, president of the Drovers' Deposit National Bank, and is a former president of the Chicago Board of Education. These disclosures caused a great stir....

On April 5 Mr. Funk was called to the stand.... The committee, the spectators and the newspaper correspondents realized that a critical moment was at hand. They hardly breathed. Mr. Funk took his seat with a determined air, and after stating his occupation as general manager of the International Harvester Company, which next to United States Steel and Standard Oil, is perhaps the greatest corporation in the country, unfolded his story. It was the first bit of testimony that has ever penetrated the surface and has given an inkling of whence came the finances for the election of Lorimer....

The whole complexion of affairs changed. The U.S. Senate further investigated Lorimer's conduct and with reluctance concluded in July 1912 that he should be deprived of his seat.

William N. Roach

In 1893 Democrat William N. Roach entered the Senate as a member from North Dakota. He came from the little town of Larimore where he was a successful small businessman via U.S. mail contracts and real estate operations. He also served as cashier for Citizens Bank of Washington, North Dakota, near Fargo. As he prepared to take his U.S. Senate seat he got into trouble when he was alleged to have embezzled $60,000 from the bank where he was an officer. Supposedly officials agreed to refrain from prosecuting him if he gave back the loot. A movement to expel him from the Senate foundered when that body determined that it could not hold a

Part 2. Election of Senators by State Legislatures

member responsible for his conduct prior to joining the Senate. In Roach's case thirteen years had elapsed between his banking offense and election to the Senate.

Marcus Hanna

"Some men must rule; the great mass of men must be ruled," Marcus Hanna declared. "Some men must own; the great mass of men must work for those who own."

William McKinley's successful 1896 campaign to be elected President was masterminded by Marcus Hanna. He invented campaign gimmicks such as drinking mugs and lapel buttons, and he blanketed the country with newsletters printed in assorted languages. He was an expert in turning problems into advantages. When McKinley's invalid wife was unable to campaign for her husband, Hanna brought the campaign to McKinley, inventing the "front porch" campaign with thousands of voters traveling to McKinley's home instead of McKinley crisscrossing the nation. Hanna sought a U.S. Senate seat from Ohio as a reward. There being no seat available, President McKinley created one by appointing Sen. John Sherman (brother of the Civil War general) Secretary of State. This created an opening for Hanna in the federal Ohio delegation, and President McKinley convinced Ohio's governor to appoint Hanna to the vacancy. Hanna took office in March 1897.

Marcus Hanna (Library of Congress).

Senators Beholden to the People

Later the state legislature elected Hanna to a full six-year term which began in 1898, the election being particularly acrimonious, with a number of Republican state legislators cooperating with Democrats, voting for the Democratic candidate rather than "Uncle Mark" Hanna. The atmosphere was similar to the outrage directed against "faithless" members of the Electoral College who vote for someone other than the presidential candidate to whom they are pledged. Some legislators were kidnapped and held until the vote was called. "Armed guards were stationed every important point. The State House was full of desperate and determined men."[33] Hanna won by one vote. In 1900, several months into his six-year term, and based on voluminous investigation, an Ohio legislature committee informed the U.S. Senate of accusations that Hanna had bribed his way into the Senate. James R. Garfield, son of the murdered President, reported that he had been told by one Republican from Cleveland that Garfield had to vote the right way, else his city pavement contracts would be

This cartoon from July 28, 1897, *Puck* magazine referring to the 1896 presidential election is captioned "Shylock Hanna—He is bound to have his pound of flesh." "Shylock Hanna" displays a document saying, "Understanding between Wm. McKinley and Mark Hanna. The aforesaid Mark Hanna shall have the Dictation of all Ohio Appointments, etc., etc." He carries a bag of boodle and a patronage knife (Library of Congress).

Part 2. Election of Senators by State Legislatures

eliminated. On advice from his attorneys Senator Hanna refused to cooperate with the Ohio investigators and portrayed the proceedings as biased against him.

The U.S. Senate responded with an investigation of its own. That Senate committee's Republican majority reported that a bribe had indeed been offered to a state legislator but that Hanna had no involvement. The Democratic minority on the U.S. Senate committee reported that transcripts of telephone conversations between the briber and Hanna headquarters were nonetheless suspicious. Hanna volunteered to testify, but the Senate committee recommended that no further investigation be made.[34] The finding was partly based on belief that nothing was to be gained through further inquiry and partly because Hanna's colleagues were uneasy about what close inquiry into Hanna's conduct might reveal about their own behavior.

David Turpie

Sen. David Turpie (D–IN) was called a "redoubtable Ajax" who "upon the stump ... struck powerful blows; his invectives, rapartees and retorts were something wonderful, ... and he used both mercilessly." In the Senate he confronted an unusual allegation. Democrats had a majority in the Indiana state legislature, and Republicans said the Democrats prevented a Republican legislator from voting, thereby swinging the U.S. Senate election to Turpie, and in addition, a Democratic legislator voted despite being ineligible to cast a ballot. Turpie's opponents declared the Senate election was therefore invalid. Senators who investigated the situation approached it as a question of who was entitled to be an Indiana legislator, an issue normally beyond the Senate's mandate. The U.S. Senate ceased its proceedings involving Turpie's right to a seat.

Alexander Caldwell

In 1871 the Kansas legislature elected banker rand railroad man Alexander Caldwell (R–KS) to the U.S. Senate. He had found a way to avoid much of the bother in running for a U.S. Senate seat. He quietly paid competitors to drop out of their campaigns and leave the way clear for him. For example, former governor Thomas Carney acknowledged that he took $15,000 to call off his 1871 Senate campaign. This technique was an innovation in corruption. Investigation by his Senate colleagues indicated that he would be forced out of office either by expulsion or by a finding that the election had been invalid. He resigned in March 1873 before action could be taken. Buddies of Caldwell said they had heard him say he had spent $60,000 on the election, an astonishing sum in that era. Friends said he was willing to spend $250,000. A Senate investigating committee unanimously declared Caldwell had bribed Kansas legislators. Referring to the Caldwell, campaign U.S. Sen. Oliver Morton (R–IN) called it "so insulting and dishonoring, showed a consciousness of guilt and demoralization that would hardly be believed if it were not well attested by history." The committee observed that Caldwell might be excused somewhat because he may not have realized his conduct was unacceptable.[35]

Stanley Matthews

Railroad attorney Stanley Matthews (R–OH) served in the Senate from 1877 to 1879 and was counsel for Rutherford Hayes on the commission examining Louisiana's electoral votes cast in the hotly contested presidential contest of 1877. (The election was held in 1876, but the commission met in 1877.) A Louisiana resident named James Anderson testified before the U.S. House of Representatives that not only had Matthews conducted himself in a fraudulent way while performing his duties but he had also promised Anderson a government job if he would help hide Matthews's illegal activity regarding the election.

A Senate investigating committee sought Anderson's testimony, but he turned out to be a reluctant witness who evaded summons from the investigators. As an alternative the committee relied on a transcript of Anderson's House testimony. Matthews appeared in person for questioning by his Senate colleagues and said he had agreed to seek a small federal job for Anderson as a reward for years of Republican activism. For unclear reasons Anderson left a false confession of

Part 2. Election of Senators by State Legislatures

wrong-doing in Matthews's safe-keeping. Two days before Matthews's Senate term expired the investigators announced his conduct in Louisiana was blameless but that he made an error in judgment in offering to help find a job for Anderson.

Roscoe Conkling

Senators Roscoe Conkling and Thomas Platt were New York Republicans feuding with President James Garfield. In a distinctly hostile act Garfield made one of Conkling's enemies Collector of the Port of New York, one of the nation's plum patronage appointments. In protest Conkling decided to resign from the Senate, and he convinced machine Republican leader Thomas Platt to join him. The idea was the New York state legislature would immediately send them back to the U.S. Senate, an action that would demonstrate machine strength and weaken Garfield in New York.

As it turned out Conkling had less influence over the New York legislature than he believed, and its members needed to vote fifty-six times before they could choose two candidates to take Conkling's and Platt's seats. The new Senators were Elbridge Lapham and Warner Miller. Conkling alleged that Lapham and Miller had won office via corrupt measures. Senate investigators disagreed, and the two were sworn in.

The Value of a Senate Seat

Large sums that some U.S. Senators either accepted or sought give an inkling of how much money a Senate seat was worth to supplicants and incumbents both. The brief examples here, of course, only cover some Senators who got caught. And in the 1990s middle class and poor voters had no more influence than they had 100 years earlier, nor did the public award Congress higher esteem at either time. For sure, the U.S. Senate was never a bastion against corruption regardless of how U.S. Senators were chosen.

An observer of the senatorial scene at the opening of the twentieth century declared,

Senators Beholden to the People

This cartoon argues that bosses of the Senate are not citizens but rather are the bloated steel trust, copper trust, Standard Oil trust, coal trust, steel beam trust, sugar trust, salt trust, and even paper bag trust. A wide entrance marled "MONOPOLISTS" welcomes their presence, while the obscure door to the second floor public visitors galley is locked and barred. The Progressive movement hoped the Seventeenth Amendment would reduce such influence (*Puck*, January 23, 1889, Library of Congress).

The scheme of looting the public domain is merely a by-product of the general system of plunder running riot throughout the country. The same tools are used upon all occasions where it is found expedient to rob the people. The same Courts are tampered with, the same members of both branches of Congress are in line, and the same heads of Departments in Washington are polluted each time, until it has come to be regarded as certain that vast interests have fattened on the life-blood of the nation by process of having a veteran force at their constant command. It goes to show that there is a close bond between the plunderers of every description, upon the same principle that there is honor among thieves, and they have developed a vein of activity in this country that has its parallel in the history of the downfall of the Roman Empire.

No nation can long survive the reign of corruption that has characterized the speculative craze existing in America during the past decade. It has permeated all branches of public service, and the history of the land

Part 2. Election of Senators by State Legislatures

frauds of the West is the history of corruptive tactics in other directions. Corruption is a hydra-headed monster of hideous mien, and the fact that it has been exposed wholesale by the land fraud trials in Oregon, and the graft prosecutions in San Francisco, and in retail fashion in other States and other cities, should never be accepted that it is dead beyond all power of resurrection.[36]

As we have seen, during Lincoln's lifetime U.S. Senators were chosen by state legislatures. For decades occasional proposals were made for voters to elect Senators by direct popular vote, excluding state legislatures from any role. A movement in this direction emerged during the late 1800s as Progressives gained influence in the Republican Party.

One important difference in the U.S. Constitution between the pre– and post–Seventeenth Amendment eras is that the pre–Seventeenth era state legislatures routinely deadlocked on choosing a U.S. Senator. An open seat might remain open for months, even for years. The state might thereby be without half (and sometimes even all) of its U.S. Senate delegation for an indefinite period. After the people began to elect U.S. Senators open seats soon disappeared.

Another difference prior to the Seventeenth Amendment is that a legislative program set by the governor and legislative leaders before the legislature convened could be stalled for weeks while legislators fussed about the U.S. Senate election, the U.S. Senator contest having priority over other legislative business. Often the delay in choosing a U.S. Senator was due to the relative strength of political parties or factions, which in turn was a factor that changed little as months or years passed. And electing a U.S. Senator was often an ordeal that state legislators had to endure again and again. Both in Lincoln's time and for decades afterward, members of a state general assembly were often serving their first term and had little experience to draw upon for handling major disputes such as electing a U.S. Senator.

Such inexperience was also a factor in holding U.S. Senators accountable for their actions. If half the state legislature wasn't running for reelection, desires of those departing legislators could be disregarded by U.S. Senators.

Senators Beholden to the People

Thus, although the notion is counter intuitive (as politicians normally seek to hold every ounce of power they can obtain), some state legislators were ready to pass the U.S. Senate election responsibility on to someone else. And that feeling was obtaining organized support from the Progressive movement, which was ready for the public to take on the responsibility at the same time that some state legislatures were ready to give it up.

Modern scholarship finds that ordinary voters and state legislators had about the same interests in choosing U.S. Senators. Regardless of whether the general electorate or the state legislature made the decision, the same kind of candidate was chosen.

Often that candidate fed off the strength of state and municipal political bosses, gentlemen for whom patronage jobs were more important than disputing about foreign affairs or a cattle disease. Some political organizations were ephemeral and disappeared after a candidate had his run in an election. Some had institutional longevity (such as Tammany Hall in New York) and remained a power to contend with regardless of who won or lost. Nineteenth-century Pennsylvania boss Matthew Quay aptly described the situation as "the art of taking money from the few and votes from the many under the pretext of protecting the one from the other."[37]

Although some Senators accused of corruption were exonerated, the charges gave the Senate a sleazy atmosphere that harmed its public standing among many citizens. Think of the saying "Where there's smoke there's fire." Accusations of bribery tended to be in connection with U.S. Senate elections conducted by state legislatures, and Progressives hoped that changing the Constitution to select Senators by popular vote would curtail corruption in elections to the Senate.

We have seen how the doctrine of instruction influenced the kind of democratic government familiar to Lincoln. And we have seen how U.S. Senators were chosen by state legislatures before the Seventeenth Amendment modified the U.S. Constitution. We shall now see how Lincoln himself sought a U.S. Senate seat using the pre–Seventeenth Amendment rules and see his invention of a way around those rules.

Part 3

Lincoln's Experiences with U.S. Senate Campaigns

Having examined the doctrine of instruction and the election of U.S. Senators by state legislatures, we can better understand Abraham Lincoln's maneuvers when he decided to run for the U.S. Senate in 1854. In an earlier book I told the story of Lincoln's 1854 campaign for the Senate. An important difference between my earlier account and this one is that this one deals with instructions received from citizens by Lincoln and other candidates, similar to what all Senate candidates experienced in that era throughout the country. If not for Lincoln's later notoriety, his two senatorial efforts (in 1854 and 1858) would be forgotten, although they contained examples of every abuse that the Progressive movement sought to remedy around 1912, from insider horse-trading of offices to bribery.

Normally U.S. Senate elections in Illinois and elsewhere dealt more with issues such as rivers and harbors than with questions of state. In 1854, however, Democrat U.S. Sen. Stephen Douglas of Illinois decided to lead the slave power's repeal of the long-standing Missouri Compromise, which banned slavery west of Missouri to the Rockies and up to Canada. Abraham Lincoln became incensed, as this repeal not only opened this vast expanse to slavery but also voided some long-standing agreements between slave states and free states.

"We were thunderstruck and stunned," Lincoln said. "We reeled and fell in utter confusion. But we rose each fighting, grasping whatever he could first reach—a scythe—a pitchfork—chopping axe, or a butcher's cleaver."[1]

Senators Beholden to the People

Throughout the North an earthquake shifted the political landscape. Suddenly the political question dividing Americans was no longer whether they favored Whigs or Democrats but whether they wanted to promote expansion of slavery. Both parties began breaking apart. The state's premier Whig newspaper, the *Illinois Daily Journal*, declared, "Everywhere is anger, distrust, and indignation."[2]

When Lincoln decided to run for the U.S. Senate, politicians in other states were also running to be selected by their state legislatures. Lincoln wasn't working in a political vacuum. Those other campaigns affected his. Douglas and President Pierce decided to make repeal of the Missouri Compromise a test of Democratic party loyalty. Any Democrat who failed to support repeal would be expelled from the party. That included not only elected officials but also newspaper editors dependent on government advertising, postmasters dependent on post office fees, government land office employees, and any other patronage positions.

Democrats throughout the country were particularly upset because the Missouri Compromise had never been an issue, so incumbents and their competitors had never received instructions from state legislators or ordinary voters. This split the Democratic Party throughout the nation. As the main Whig newspaper in Illinois put it, "It is a surprise upon the country. No one called for it; no one looked for it, no one dreamed of it."[3] From Alton, Illinois, Democrat and former U.S. Representative John McClernand shouted, "Why should fealty to repeal of the Missouri Compromise be made a Democratic test?.... That Compromise stood upon the statute book for more than thirty years."[4] Jurisdictions that had been safely Democrat for years now became battlegrounds. This was an opportunity that Whigs might not have again for a long time.

Fortunately for Douglas, he was not up for reelection in 1854; the famed Lincoln–Douglas debates were several years in the future. In 1854 Lincoln officially wanted to replace Democratic U.S. Senator James Shields. Shields was vulnerable, spending much of his time with big shots in Washington rather than returning to Illinois when he had an opportunity to mend political fences. Lincoln and Shields were longtime political and personal opponents.

Part 3. Lincoln's Experiences with U.S. Senate Campaigns

Douglas's Democratic opponents in Illinois, who called themselves "Independent" Democrats, began cooperating with Whigs who had not known how to stay in public life as their party died off but now received a reprieve by battling Douglas's repeal of the Missouri Compromise. In the election for U.S. Representative in the fifth congressional district, Lincoln's Whig friend Archie Williams almost beat Douglas's ally William Richardson. The eighth district was the home of James Shields, who warned, "There is no hope for this district. All is perfect chaos. And the feeling is such that no effort can accomplish anything. Two things have contributed to putting seal upon this district. The *test*, as they call it, of Douglas to make men acknowledge that the [repeal of the Missouri Compromise by the Kansas-Nebraska] Act was all right and the other the exposition of [Missouri Democrat Sen. Dave] Atchison—that he wanted [Kansas to be a] slave state back of Missouri [in Missouri Compromise territory] and that Douglas consented to be his instrument to effect this."[5] "Independent" Democrat Lyman Trumbull soared to victory in the eighth.

Lincoln took the unusual approach of campaigning with "Invincible Dick" Yates who was running for sixth district Congressman. The two coordinated their travels together, sometimes splitting up to campaign in towns, meeting up again later on. Throughout the Yates campaign, whenever Lincoln spoke he concentrated on the Missouri Compromise rather than normal Western issues such as tariffs or federal aid for improving river transportation. Keep in mind that as 1854 progressed Lincoln was not yet openly running for any elective office, but in a controversy he liked to concentrate on one issue and shape the discussion around it. Although Lincoln was helping Yates in the summer, Lincoln was also preparing voters for the issue he wanted state legislators to focus on when choosing a new U.S. Senator in the coming winter, namely, expansion of slavery.

Lincoln was probably the most prominent Whig politician in Illinois, having served in the U.S. House of Representatives and campaigned for President Zachary Taylor in the Northeast section of the country (a service for which Taylor, in thanks, offered Lincoln the governorship of Oregon Territory, a vast district much larger than the later state). Taylor probably would have given Lincoln the plum appointment of commissioner of the General Land Office in Washington (in charge of distributing land to settlers) if Illinois Whigs had not started fighting about which Illinois Whig faction should have priority.

Douglas tried to manipulate instructions from Illinois Democrats to maximize appearance of support for repeal of the Missouri Compromise. A Lee County meeting backfired when only five supporters of Douglas turned up; all other Democrats who attended opposed repeal of the Missouri Compromise. At first a Peoria meeting voted down all resolutions which supported Missouri Compromise repeal. Then an announcement declared the meeting was only for persons in favor of repealing the Compromise. All but sixteen departed, and thereby a handful of Peoria Democrats told Douglas to vote for his own bill. Hardly resounding support. Similar scenarios played out in county meetings across Illinois. Douglas and his allies claimed he was getting support from such gatherings, but that bragging was for public consumption. He and his followers knew they were in trouble.

Until autumn arrived in 1854, from Washington Douglas had pretty much responded to critics simply by name calling. Now his Illinois colleagues apparently helped him to understand that their necks were on the line with his, and if he wanted their continued support, he had to do more than ridicule voters who disagreed with him. Douglas headed back to Illinois on an itinerary that took him to New York, Chicago, "downstate" Illinois, and the state fair in Springfield. One of his campaign techniques was to get his crowds of listeners to pass resolutions endorsing his stances on issues. To a modern observer such conduct might seem hokey—after all, who would we expect a Douglas gathering to support? These resolutions, however, could be portrayed as instructions that Douglas had to obey.

The reception Douglas got was mixed. Lincoln stalked him for a while, addressing crowds that Douglas had raised, conduct that angered Douglas. As one of Lincoln's supporters said, "Lincoln is apt to be where he isn't wanted."[6] Lincoln advocated disruption of Douglas's speeches and publicly joked about Douglas's experience with rowdy hecklers.

Part 3. Lincoln's Experiences with U.S. Senate Campaigns

When the Yates campaign for Congress was moving along, Lincoln and his former law partner Stephen Logan each declared their candidacies for one of the seats in Springfield districts of the Illinois house of representatives. This was the unofficial opening of Lincoln's campaign for the U.S. Senate seat held by James Shields. Evidently announcement of the Lincoln and Logan campaign produced an argument between Lincoln and his wife Mary. She insisted that Abraham withdraw his state legislature candidacy. Offhand this looked foolish, as Lincoln was so popular among Whigs that his victory would be certain. This popularity was important because for the first time Whigs were close to having enough votes in the state legislature to elect someone to the U.S. Senate.

That was all fine, but there was one big problem. The Illinois constitution prohibited election of a state legislator to the U.S. Senate. This restriction probably violated the U.S. Constitution, but that point had not yet been adjudicated. Nonetheless that point quickly became one of the hottest pieces of political gossip in Illinois. Probably Mary did not want Abraham to be the test case. He realized, however, how crucial his state candidacy was for creating an anti–Douglas statehouse majority. Moreover, Lincoln's candidacy would assure a good turnout from local Whig voters, who would also vote for Logan and Yates. Still, the state constitution's provision might lose him enough legislators' votes to thwart his selection. Bean counters determined that Whigs would have a one-vote majority in U.S. Senate balloting. An ally told Lincoln, "We shall need every vote that we can muster. How shall we spare yours?"[7]

Effects of that legislative majority went beyond the senatorial choice. Because state legislators elected the U.S. Senator they could instruct him. Judging from commentary in Douglas's organ *Chicago Times*, Douglas was sweating the possibility of the Illinois legislature telling him to seek restoration of the Missouri Compromise. Indeed, Lincoln was drafting instructions in case he defeated Shields, and Douglas was scheming a way to label such instructions as invalid and therefore non-binding on him. So the one-vote anti–Nebraska majority in the Illinois was a big deal, bigger than Lincoln's fate alone.

Senators Beholden to the People

This provision of the state constitution was not some unnoticed obscurity. In the 1849 U.S Senate election it had been cited as preventing Whig legislators from voting for state representative Usher Linder and in 1853 as forbidding state senator Jo Gillespie from running against Shields. A supporter from Peoria advised Lincoln, "It has been talked of here amongst some of us as your being the choice for Senator, and the fact of your ineligibility has been mentioned, which will have a tendency to injure your prospects."[8] What was more important—a surefire Lincoln victory running for the state legislature, which would guarantee Whig control of that body, or a riskier campaign for U.S. Senator, in which the state constitution might disqualify him from serving in Washington?

Lincoln decided to give up his seat in the state general assembly. This was in November 1854 when state legislators were being voted on by the general electorate, not a time when the legislature was voting for U.S. Senator, but Lincoln soon started a canvass of legislators. Local Whig leaders chose Norman Broadwell to be their candidate in the special state legislature election as the substitute for replacing Lincoln. Broadwell had studied law in the Lincoln & Herndon law office. After Broadwell set up his law practice, in 1852 he ran against Herndon for eighth judicial circuit attorney. Herndon withdrew from the contest to give Broadwell a clear track, a big favor to Broadwell. What local Whig leaders didn't know in 1854 was that he had come a Whig opponent.

The official Democratic candidate won, and among Democrats there was much jollification. From Washington a dismayed Whig Congressman, Elihu Washburne, wrote to Lincoln, "There is much rejoicing among the Loco Focos [Democrats] in the U.S. House today on the report that your county has elected a Loco Foco Nebraskaite in your place. They now claim the election of Shields as certain."[9] Forthright admission that county Whig leaders inadvertently ran a Lincoln opponent was awkward. Two of Lincoln's White House assistants recalled, "Whigs in other parts of the state were furious ..., and the incident served greatly to complicate the senatorial canvass."[10]

Yates lost reelection to Congress by 200 votes, the kind of result

Part 3. Lincoln's Experiences with U.S. Senate Campaigns

that might ordinarily have cost Lincoln some sleep (that is, if he didn't stay awake brooding about Whig William Archer's loss of the seventh district congressional seat by one vote).

If Whigs elected Lincoln to replace the Democrat U.S. Sen. James Shields, that action would put one of Douglas's toughest opponents (Lincoln) in a position to attack Douglas every day on the floor of the U.S. Senate. This scenario sounded good not only to Illinois Whigs but also to anti–Nebraska "Independent" Democratic legislators such as Silas Ramsey, who told Lincoln, "Our views in regard to political matters correspond, and we should most likely be found acting together."[11]

In September a Quincy Whig wrote Lincoln, "All the Whigs here would be much gratified if you could make it convenient and pay us a visit while the Little Giant [Douglas nickname] is here ... and thereby create a debt of gratitude on the part of the Whigs here, which they may at some time, have it in their power, to repay with pleasure and with interest."[12] Here we can perceive a promise of support for higher office, and the only one available was the U.S. Senate.

Later in the month Lincoln received a letter from McDonough County: "Douglas is here at court (next Monday week). We are anxious to have someone here to hold him in check.... We know of no one who would be more eagerly listened to than yourself.... Your name is also spoke of as a candidate for U.S. Senator. Can we not reasonably hope to elect a thorough anti–Nebraska legislature? If so we hope for your election to that place.... Come if possible; by so doing you will place the Whigs under renewed obligation to you."[13]

We begin to see a reason beyond altruism for Lincoln campaigning across the sixth Congressional district as a surrogate for Yates, for speech-making outside that district, for challenging Douglas face to face again and again, for thereby placing anti–Nebraska legislators across the state in his debt, and for hesitating to seek an Illinois house of representatives seat that would help guarantee an anti–Nebraska legislature but interfere with making him the legislature's choice for U.S. Senator.

As autumn approached, the influential George Gage, who was about to become a state senator from the Chicago area, kept Lincoln informed about what other prominent officials were doing: "The Hon. E.B. Washburne is not mistaken with regard to my preferences for our U.S.A. Senator, and I think I have most of the members from this part of the state with me.... Rest assured you have my best wishes, and I shall try and render you all the assistance I can."[14]

As Lincoln's Whig base was solid, everything he did in the autumn campaign should be viewed as intended to further his credibility among anti–Nebraska Democratic legislators who might cross over and vote for the right Whig.

He responded instantly when he received a report that his presence at an event was vital. At the end of October Horace White told him, "Chicago has five votes in the legislature and influences a great many more in northern Illinois.... The idea is to have you go to Chicago and make a speech. You will have a crowd of from eight to ten or fifteen thousand and the result will be that the people will demand of their representatives to elect a Whig Senator [possibly through instruction]. What might be doubtful otherwise will thus be rendered certain."[15] Two days later Lincoln spoke in Chicago. He spoke past 10:00 p.m., then headed for Urbana where Champaign County Circuit Court was convening—occasioning still more speaking.

He was receiving reports of legislators' predilections. "I saw Mr. Coffing from Peru and from him learned that Day was probably in favor of Mr. Sweet."[16] "I have seen Mr. Sullivan.... He will act together with the Whig Party in regard to Senator."[17] Lincoln engaged in intensive lobbying with frankness that could be damaging if revealed. Again and again he told correspondents, "Let this be confidential." "Don't let *anyone* know I have written you this." "Do not speak of the Nebraska letter mentioned above." Reportedly he asked some recipients to destroy the correspondence after reading.[18]

Lincoln received many assurances of support. "Courtney's promise to go for you was made a condition precedent to his election."[19] Lincoln even did candidate recruiting to put more of his supporters in the state legislature, advising all to emphasize any local issues they could find (such as roads) and to go lightly on Kansas-Nebraska.

Lincoln's increasing popular support promoted his standing

Part 3. Lincoln's Experiences with U.S. Senate Campaigns

among legislators who felt they had to obey the doctrine of instruction. A Peoria supporter wrote, "People generally in this region are directed to you as 'the Man.'"[20] "It will be perfectly in accordance with my personal views and so far as I am able to judge, also of those who elected me, support you for the U.S.S."[21] Lincoln received word that "our people here are all for you, and if necessary we can get up a public meeting, to instruct our representatives and senators."[22] Illinois Whigs were becoming excited: "A Whig U.S. Senator!!! Hold me, or I shall burst."[23]

Then there was the matter of convincing "Independent" Democratic legislators to vote for a Whig. "I would commence trading at once with the anti–Nebraska Democrats. I would give them everything."[24] Plenty of free advice was available to Lincoln on implementing this strategy. "Everyone believes that by giving away all but Senator we can unite all the anti–Nebraska force."[25]

When Lincoln sent a feeler to independent Democrat Thomas Turner, Turner responded, "I am not committed to anyone for the office of U.S. Senator, nor do I intend to be until I know where I can exert my influence the most successfully against those who are seeking to extend the era of slavery."[26] Elihu Washburne advised Lincoln that Turner "would like to be speaker of the [Illinois] house. This is worth looking to."[27] Lincoln's ally David Davis suggested to Lincoln, "Had you not better urge your friends to elect, say, Turner speaker…. Burn this letter."[28] Douglas's supporters believed Turner was inclined toward reelecting incumbent U.S. Senator Shields who was pro–Nebraska, and Douglas's forces, too, noted Turner's thirst to be speaker. Turner was elected speaker of the house with Whig support, and when balloting for U.S. Senator was to start, Lincoln's floor manager Stephen Logan made the resolution to elect Lincoln. Turner then showed his true colors and declined to vote for Lincoln, earning a public denunciation from Logan.

Shields took what passed for a moderate stance in that time: "Where there are two distinct races in the same community, one inferior and one superior, like the negro and the white race, a state of mild and gentle slavery is the safest and happiest condition for the inferior race."[29] His Senate vote favoring Douglas's Kansas-Nebraska Act made him a target of every anti–Nebraska force in Illinois.

The sharks inhabiting Illinois political waters scented his blood, and rather than come to Shields's aid, Democrat politicians treated his peril as opportunity to take his Senate seat. But he contributed to his defeat by running a lackadaisical reelection campaign, apparently not even seeking an elementary report on the legislature's makeup until the last days of November, when his competitors had already been lobbying legislators for weeks. Douglas decided to jump in by directing allies to argue that Whigs opposed Shields because he was an Irish Catholic immigrant. (Interestingly, Shields became a Lincoln & Herndon law firm client.) Shields's two main Democrat competitors were state supreme court justice Lyman Trumbull and business executive Joel Matteson.

Trumbull had just gotten himself elected to the U.S. House of Representatives and acknowledged that immediately seeking a U.S. Senate seat looked bad. In the House campaign, however, he had become the champion of independent Democrats, who opposed Douglas and the Nebraska bill. Douglas supporters wanted Trumbull expelled from the Democratic Party. Trumbull expressed shock at the depth of anger expressed by some Democrats. "They would, some of them, sooner vote for a Whig."[30]

Three weeks before the legislature balloted for Senator, a Douglas lieutenant wrote, "All hope of electing Shields is gone."[31] The Illinois Democratic establishment was shifting from Shields to former governor Joel Matteson.

Democrats put off the U.S. Senate election as long as they could, as delay gave opportunity to whip up more public hatred of abolitionists, which could be aimed at Lincoln. Reportedly Trumbull supporters spread a damaging report that prominent Ohio abolitionist Joshua Giddings was urging Illinois abolitionists to line up for Lincoln. The claim was true. Conversely Illinois abolitionist leader Zebina Eastman was saying Lincoln's stance on slavery wasn't good enough.

Lincoln went on the offensive, drafting instructions for the general assembly to give Douglas. These required Douglas to seek

Part 3. Lincoln's Experiences with U.S. Senate Campaigns

reenactment of the Missouri Compromise, prevent the Territories of Kansas and Nebraska from being admitted to the Union as slave states, prevent extension of slavery into anyplace currently free, and maintain the illegality of the African slave trade.

In Springfield the U.S. Senate balloting was scheduled for February 8, 1855. Lincoln feared he was three votes short and was clueless about where those three would come from. As voting progressed Matteson built strength. All sides pressured the five Independent Democrat supporters of Trumbull, but they wouldn't budge and refused to vote for the Whig Lincoln. A two-hour lunch break was called for players to regroup. Lincoln was ahead in the voting, but Matteson was gaining fast, with Trumbull supporters starting to appear from nowhere.

Although key Lincoln supporters wanted to persevere, the professional politician in Lincoln saw that the choice was now between Douglas's ally Matteson or anti–Nebraska man Trumbull. Part of Lincoln's certainty that he had to drop out lest Matteson win was based on a report from a spy who eavesdropped on Matteson supporters arranging a bribe. Lincoln ordered his own supporters to switch to Trumbull, and the anti–Nebraska Democrat Trumbull won immediately. He would go on to become one of Lincoln's staunchest allies. Lincoln's law partner Billy Herndon shrugged and said privately that Trumbull was a "great thorn, rough and poisonous, in the heart of Douglas."[32]

In 1855 a legislator told Lincoln that they would win when the next Senate election was held. Lincoln "replied ... that before that time the taste for the senatorship would get out of his mouth."[33]

But the taste remained in his mouth, and in 1858 Lincoln tried again. Perhaps the greatest hurdle for him to clear was Democrat gerrymandering of state legislature districts.[34] If U.S. Senators were elected by popular vote (as Progressives would advocate fifty years later) each candidate for Senator would run at large, with gerrymandered state legislative boundary maps becoming irrelevant for selecting a U.S. Senator. But that would not happen until Amendment Seventeen was added to the U.S. Constitution in the twentieth century.

Senators Beholden to the People

Lincoln reversed the advice he gave to his supporters last time. In 1854 he recommended that they go easy on slavery matters and try to direct voter attention to typical issues of concern to Western residents. Now organizing in depth, Lincoln advised, "From the poll books in the county clerk's office, you have made alphabetical lists of all the voters in each precinct ... the lists to be in separate letter books, and to be corrected, by striking off such as may have died or removed, and adding such as will be entitled to vote at the next election.... You see how, like a map, it lays the whole field before you. You know, at once, *how*, and with *whom* to work."[35] In October 1857 Lincoln and others called a convention to nominate candidates for county office on the basis of their stance on national issues. The question was not whether hopefuls would be a good coroner or sheriff or legislator but how they stood on Kansas-Nebraska.

In 1858 Lincoln decided that he would not wait for the legislative election to choose the legislators that he would have to lobby. Instead he would go to the people. A hundred Republican county conventions were held to select delegates to the state convention, and ninety-five gatherings unanimously passed resolutions endorsing Lincoln for U.S. Senator. His supporters thereby got the Illinois state convention to make him the Republican party's unanimous nominee for U.S. Senator. He transformed the U.S. Senate choice into the overriding issue of every state legislator campaign. Roads, bridges, banks, schools, and every other normal issue receded into irrelevancy. In 1858 the only question a general assembly candidate had to answer was "Who will get your vote for U.S. Senator?" Lincoln would not go cap in hand to legislators as he did in 1854, a supplicant pleading for favor. In 1858 he would send their constituents after them, making their office-holding dependent on what they promised voters about Lincoln. Fear is a great motivator, and Lincoln had devised a way to make general assembly candidates fear him.

His strategy was legal but clearly violated the spirit of the Constitution's provision about state legislators electing Senators. Assorted commentators expressed alarm about Lincoln's innovation. The *Philadelphia Pennsylvanian* spoke of a "revolutionary effort to destroy the

Part 3. Lincoln's Experiences with U.S. Senate Campaigns

true intent and spirit of the Constitution."[36] Douglas himself mused, "It has never been usual for any party, or any convention to nominate a candidate for United States Senator."[37]

Eventually Lincoln's innovation would have horrific cost. Except for the occasional bribe, up to 1858 U.S. Senate campaigns could be run effectively for a few hundred dollars. Back-slapping and correspondence with 100 legislators cost little. After the Seventeenth Amendment to the Constitution was enacted, making Senators responsible to a state's entire electorate, millions of dollars would become necessary to reach tens of thousands of voters and run an effective campaign. And Senators' loyalty would belong to the sources of that funding.

A correspondent reminded Lincoln that "money is power, and it controls almost everything.... I want the Republicans to go to work, and buy out enough of the Douglas men so that they will not appear in the legislature.... If they will not sell out and vote for you, buy their seats."[38] Lincoln replied, "Your very kind letter ... was duly received. I shall duly consider its contents."[39] We have no indication that Lincoln implemented his correspondent's advice to go directly to Douglas legislators and bribe them. Such conduct, however, was hardly unheard of—President Buchanan himself bragged about bribing Illinois Democrats.[40] Douglas raised and spent campaign money in sums reminiscent of what plutocrats gave to U.S. Senate candidates fifty years later. Douglas was spending tens of thousands, including huge sums obtained from out of state. Reportedly New York's Tammany Society furnished $50,000. Lincoln received a private report that Tammany was willing to back Douglas with $1 million, but that sum is hard to believe.[41] Lincoln's well informed operative David Davis reported that New York City mayor Fernando Wood loaned $39,000 to the Douglas campaign and that Douglas had mortgaged Chicago property to get $13,000 more. A later report said Douglas borrowed $90,000. Apparently Douglas expended a substantial chunk on a private railroad car. Reportedly another $5,000 of his money bought editorial friendliness from the *St. Louis Republican*. A more tangible use of funds was to bring in Irish voters. The Illinois Central Railroad cooperated with that, importing hundreds of alien Douglas voters into doubtful

Senators Beholden to the People

counties who weren't residents of the county where they were illegally voting (and maybe were not even U.S. citizens).

Lincoln won the popular vote, and if the Seventeenth Amendment had been in effect, he would have gone to the U.S. Senate. But Democratic gerrymandering of state legislative districts defeated him.

As we have seen, in Lincoln's time local district voter meetings could force a dozen state representatives to demand that a Senator agree to what those 300 voters wanted. This was the spirit of democracy in action. Those 300 persons couldn't vote for Senator, but they could compel the Senator to do something. As the twenty-first century dawned a Senator could feel safe ignoring a petition from a million voters. Each of those voters could cast a direct ballot for Senator, but even in aggregate they had no influence on the Senator's actions. Stripped of influence, let alone control, ordinary voters began to view the main source of campaign funding—great corporations—as sinister.

Some elected officials (but not Lincoln) were viewed as errand boys of railway corporations. Lincoln was not a railroad employee, but he routinely represented railways in court, with this work involving important cases ranging from building a bridge across the Mississippi River despite opposition from U.S. Secretary of War Jefferson Davis to eliminating any state tax liability billed to the Illinois Central Railroad. This employment was well known and public. Not everyone felt comfortable with the company Lincoln kept.

By the 1860s railroads had started to acquire great influence in American society, enough to control state legislatures through bribery or intimidation and, by extrapolation, exercise control of the U.S. Senate. In 1857 the *Rock Island Morning Argus* told its readers, "segregated and aggregated their capital is heavy—kept under the eye of a few heads, readily at command and easily allied one with the other. The thousand and one arteries of which this great system consists, throb responsive to the throes of one gigantic heart. One brain colonizes and controls the nerves of the whole body. Touch at the right time and in a hostile manner, the minutest fiber of this vast frame, and the entire structure is aroused and with herculean force prepares for defense or attack."[42]

Such was the growing fear experienced by voters.

Part 3. Lincoln's Experiences with U.S. Senate Campaigns

As the twentieth century began, a series of articles in *Cosmopolitan* magazine titled "The Treason of the Senate" cited corrupt influence that great corporations (the Trusts) had among Senators. These articles boosted public support for exercising greater influence over the upper branch of Congress and indeed for eliminating state legislatures from any role in choosing Senators, making U.S. Senators elected directly by voters.

Popular perception that Senate seats could be bought in backrooms of state legislatures fueled support for direct elections. Reformers known as Progressives had a broader agenda than the Seventeenth Amendment's electoral reform and supported changes at federal, state, and local levels—changes like trust busting, female suffrage, beverage alcohol prohibition, ending child labor (twenty-seven million children were of school age, and more than two million of these labored in factories, shops, and mines), using initiative and referendum to change laws, non-partisan elections (replacing conventions), unicameral legislatures with (to a lesser degree) democratic election of federal judges, and making lawyers be agents of courts and be no longer allowed to charge private practice fees. Progressives also observed that class inequality was growing, half the country's wealth being owned by less than 1 percent of the population. "The Treason of the Senate" noted that "heavy and ever heavier taxes of 'the interests' are swelling rents, swelling the prices of food, clothing, fuel, all the necessities and all the necessary comforts. And the Senate both forbids the lifting of those taxes and levies fresh taxes."

Progressive Robert Owen (D–OK) called on his Senate colleagues to pay attention to what was happening on state and municipal levels as well. He noted that initiative (citizens' right to draft legislation and vote on whether to enact it into law) and referendum (right of citizens to repeal legislation adopted by a legislature) and recall (citizens' right to remove an elected official and remove judges from office) appeared in Arizona's constitution. (We have not discussed recall because the venerable procedure is familiar to Americans today, dating back at least to adoption of the 1780 Massachusetts constitution.) Owen declared:

Senators Beholden to the People

Commercial conspiracies ... have controlled cities and towns for the purpose of making money out of street railways, telephone and telegraph companies, electric light companies, water companies, municipal activities, street paving building sewerage systems, and so forth. They have undertaken the control of larger municipalities, of cities from New York, Pittsburg, St. Louis, and Denver.... I beg you to look at the disclosures in San Francisco, for example, brought about by Francis I. Heney and Rudolph Spreckles. I invite your attention to the shocking criminal conduct of the municipal management of the city of Denver set forth by Ben Lindsay in "The Beast and the Jungle." I invite your consideration of the wholesale corruption and municipal graft of St. Louis.... Do you recall that 116 men, members of the city council, leading bankers and prominent business men of Pittsburg were indicted at one time for wholesale thieving of public property under cover of law?[43]

Progressive reform in Oregon, Owen said,

has terminated corrupt practices, the buying of votes, the coercing of votes, the hiring of voters for election day, hauling voters to the polls, soliciting voters on election day; it has abated blackmail, legislative incompetency, neglect or treachery. It has made legislative or administrative officers responsive to the public will. It has made speedy and satisfactory the civil and criminal court procedure; it has established the rule of the people and enthroned the intelligence and conscience of the State in the governing business.[44]

The infamous conduct of machine politics in buying votes has been illustrated recently in Adams County, Ohio, where nearly 2,000 citizens confessed to having sold their votes and in like manner in Danville, Ill., similar disclosures are now in progress.... Men saw no hope of good government under this system.... Some great sinister force, some mighty commercial power with enormous wealth has come into the wholesale system of corrupting the citizens as well as the municipal officers, until graft is penetrating this country from the highest to the lowest, from the gigantic captains of finance, who control the power to expand the credits of the Nation or to contract the credits of the country and who make hundreds of millions at one operation, down to the cooks in our households.... The time has come to end the corruption and dishonesty of American life and the initiative and referendum is the only practicable means by which it can be speedily done.[45]

Owen proclaimed, "The issue is between government by corporations and special interests and government by the people."[46] Progressive heirs to Abraham Lincoln had set themselves quite an agenda.

Part 3. Lincoln's Experiences with U.S. Senate Campaigns

Moreover, the Seventeenth Amendment was seen as part of a broader effort to make an end-run around the control that parties, machines, and special interests had over state legislatures. (Ironically, however, big city party machines supported the Seventeenth Amendment, largely because otherwise state legislative district apportionment gave greater representation to low populated rural areas, in some cases allowing a state legislature to be elected by less than ten percent of the electorate. Plus the Seventeenth Amendment would allow machine-controlled cities to more easily mobilize voters rather than having to rely on persuasion of legislators. Many big special interests supported the Seventeenth Amendment as well.) Journalism typified by "The Treason of the Senate" and "The Shame of the Cities" played major roles in shaping debate swirling around the Seventeenth Amendment.

Various ways exist to shape government policy. In the second half of the nineteenth century experience showed that money was the most effective way for a corporation to affect senatorial election outcomes or persuade a government agency or official to approve something that a corporation wanted to do. Bribing state legislators and city council members might be more costly than paying a U.S. Senator because a state legislator had substantial power to select a U.S. Senator who served the Trusts, Trusts being most familiar "on the ground" in the form of railroads, either long haul or streetcars.

Muckraker Lincoln Steffens told the following story in *The Shame of the City*:

> That evening a conference was held in Governor Johnson's office, and the next day this story was told in the grand jury room by Charles H. Turner, millionaire president of the Suburban Railway, and corroborated by Philip Stock, man-about-town and a good fellow: The Suburban, anxious to sell out at a large profit to its only competitor, the St. Louis Transit Co., caused to be drafted the measure known as House Bill No. 44. So sweeping were its grants that Mr. Turner, who planned and executed the document, told the directors in his confidence that its enactment into law would enhance the value of the property from three to six million dollars. The bill introduced, Mr. Turner visited Colonel Butler, who had long been known as a legislative agent, and

Senators Beholden to the People

asked his price for securing the passage of the measure. "One hundred and forty-five thousand dollars will be my fee," was the reply. The railway president demurred. He would think the matter over, he said, and he hired a cheaper man, Mr. Stock. Stock conferred with the representative of the combine in the House of Delegates and reported that $75,000 would be necessary in this branch of the Assembly. Mr. Turner presented a note indorsed by two of the directors whom he could trust, and secured a loan from the German American Savings Bank.

Men ran into debt to the extent of thousands of dollars for the sake of election to either branch of the Assembly. One night, on a street car going to the City Hall, a new member remarked that the nickel he handed the conductor was his last. The next day he deposited $5,000 in a savings bank.[47]

Under prodding from Progressives a consensus grew that electing U.S. Senators by direct vote of the populace would reduce corruption, and changing the Constitution would allow good government to trickle down from the top.

Epilogue
A Modest Proposal

Does our examination of antique laws and customs have any importance beyond the antiquarian trade? Are there any lessons applicable to American democracy as we trudge deeper into the twenty-first century?

Lincoln's way of doing things had its merits and drawbacks, but it consistently sought to make government more accountable to the people. That aim was treated as desirable. The means of achieving it was debated, but no one questioned the goal itself.

This book was written at a time when Americans were losing faith in democracy, largely, I believe, because they felt cut off from exercising control over the persons and institutions that rule our lives. If such control could be restored, the chance for improving our society might increase, as traditionally most Americans have had a plain understanding of reality—although currently that trait is being exhibited less often than we might like.

If we exercise our imaginations we might see how direct democracy and representative democracy could combine to increase government accountability. Suppose once or twice a year a precinct meeting were called to discuss citizen concerns. As in the nineteenth century, a series of resolutions could be passed, summarizing the sense of the meeting on these matters. Precinct chairmen could be elected to meet later in the ward for discussing the precinct resolutions and maybe pass ward level resolutions. The ward assemblies could send a representative from each one to a meeting comprised of a congressional district. Thereby representatives of the congressional district would have

Epilogue

faced three elections to reach the top level of the pyramid. They could then elect the President of the United States.

This set-up would be a pyramid form of organization, with the numbers of participants declining as we ascend the pyramid. Also the number of constituents would decline the higher up we go. Except for the presidential election, which would require a big change in law and even in thinking, the pyramid organization would stand apart from the Constitution and could be taken on a "test drive" to see if direct democracy could still work. The test would not have to be nationwide but could be tried in just one state. Performing such an experiment could be done while retaining our congressional set-up, simply to see if direct democracy can compete with representative democracy today. The policy of resignation of Senators and Representatives would not have to first be codified in law, any more than it was in the 1800s. Indeed, when this book was written, some state constitutions, such as those of North Carolina, Nevada, and Kansas, still contained provisions guaranteeing voters' right to instruct their representatives.

An important element of pyramid organization is that each meeting would be human-size, and persons elected by meetings would have human-size constituencies, producing a blend of direct and representative democracy. As someone ascends in the pyramid the constituencies wouldn't increase in size but accountability would, and the government would become less direct and more representative.

The point of this epilogue is to illustrate that the doctrine of instruction could be implemented again if desired, although the form it would take is unknown. I hope readers' understanding of both Lincoln and his time are promoted by this examination.

Chapter Notes

Part One

1. John Adams diary, v. 3 Papers, v. 1, Sept. 24, 1765, https://www.masshist.org/publications/adams-papers/index.php/view/ADMS-06-01-02-0054-0003#sn=48.

2. *Massachusetts Gazette*, Oct. 10, 1765, quoted in John Adams Papers, https://www.masshist.org/publications/adams-papers/index.php/view/ADMS-06-01-02-0054-0004#sn=50.

3. William Tudor to John Adams, Sept. 22, 1774, John Adams Papers, https://www.masshist.org/publications/adams-papers/index.php/view/ADMS-06-02-02-0047#sn=114.

4. John Niles, *Congressional Globe*, 25:2, July 2, 1838, p. 467.

5. *Congressional Globe*, 26:1, June 17, 1840, p. 470.

6. *Congressional Globe*, 27:1, June 22, 1841, p. 89.

7. Burgh, *Political*, book 4, 181.

8. Prof. Peverill Squire has a distinguished academic career in political science, with an emphasis on state legislatures. See in particular his *The Right of Instruction and Representation in American Legislatures, 1778 to 1900*.

9. John Adams to James Burgh, Dec. 28, 1774, Founders Online, U.S. National Archives, https://founders.archives.gov/documents/Adams/06-02-02-0066. See A. Roane, "Right of Instruction," *Southern Literary Messenger* 2 (Oct. 1836): 687 ff., and *Annals of Congress*, 1:1, Aug. 15, 1789, 761 ff., segment on whether instruction should be included in U.S. Constitution,.

10. *Annals of Congress*, 1:1, Aug. 15, 1789, 765; Burgh, *Political*, 185.

11. Pennsylvania Assembly, Reply to Governor, Aug. 19, 1755, Benjamin Franklin Papers, "Pennsylvania Assembly: Reply to the Governor, 19 August 1755," *Founders Online*, U.S. National Archives, https://founders.archives.gov/documents/Franklin/01-06-02-0069.

12. Richard Jackson: Private Sentiments and Advice on Pennsylvania Affairs, April 24, 1758, Benjamin Franklin Papers, https://franklinpapers.org/framedVolumes.jsp.

13. The Privy Council: Order on Franklin's Petition, Wed., Aug. 29, 1759, Benjamin Franklin Papers, https://franklinpapers.org/framedVolumes.jsp.

14. Burgh, *Political*, 181.

15. Burgh, *Political*, 183.

16. Burgh, *Political*, 183, 196.

17. Quoted in A. Roane, "Right of Instruction," *Southern Literary Messenger* 2 (Oct. 1836): 687.

18. Quoted in A. Roane, "Right of Instruction," *Southern Literary Messenger* 2 (Oct. 1836): 687.

19. *Congressional Globe*, 25:2, p. 190; *Congressional Globe*, weekly ed., 27:1, June 18, 1841, p. 88.

20. Quoted in *Congressional Globe*, 25:3, Jan. 14, 1839, p. 110.

21. Quoted in A. Roane, "Right of Instruction," *Southern Literary Messenger* 2 (Oct. 1836): 688. This description

Notes—Part One

applied the British experience to America.

22. *Congressional Globe*, 31:3, 1854, p. 445.

23. *Congressional Globe*, 26:2, Feb. 19, p. 196.

24. Eliott's *Debates*, 1:68.

25. "A Declaration of the Rights of the Inhabitants of the Commonwealth or State of Pennsylvania."

26. New York Assembly *Journal*, resolution on the call of a convention of the states, Feb. 17, 1787.

27. Quoted in A. Roane, "Right of Instruction," *Southern Literary Messenger* 2 (Oct. 1836): 687.

28. Hamilton to King, Jan. 29, 1796.

29. Jefferson to Carmichael, June 3, 1788.

30. New York Ratifying Convention, First Speech of June 21, 1788 (Francis Childs's Version), quoted in A. Roane, "Right of Instruction," *Southern Literary Messenger* 2 (Oct. 1836): 687.

31. Quoted in A. Roane, "Right of Instruction," *Southern Literary Messenger* 2 (Oct. 1836): 687.

32. Quoted in Massaro, *No Guarantee*, 398.

33. *Journal* of the Senate of the United States of America, 1789–1793, Rhode Island ratification declaration, 1790, 159, 335.

34. Quoted in Massaro, *No Guarantee*, 398.

35. Alexander Hamilton to William Livingston, Aug. 29, 1788.

36. June 12, 1776.

37. June 27, 1788, both quoted in A. Roane, "Right of Instruction," *Southern Literary Messenger* 2 (Oct. 1836): 688.

38. Quoted in A. Roane, "Right of Instruction," *Southern Literary Messenger* 2 (Oct. 1836): 688, and in https://avalon.law.yale.edu/18th_century/ratnc.asp.

39. *Annals of Congress*, 1:1, Aug. 15, 1789, 761 ff.

40. *Annals of Congress*, 1:1, Aug. 15, 1789, p. 760.

41. *Annals of Congress*, 1:1, Aug. 15, 1789, p. 761.

42. *Annals of Congress*, 1:1, Aug. 15, 1789, p. 762.

43. *Annals of Congress*, 1:1, Aug. 15, 1789, p. 763.

44. *Annals of Congress*, 1:1, Aug. 15, 1789, pp. 763–64.

45. *Annals of Congress*, 1:1, Aug. 15, 1790, p. 736.

46. https://www.tsl.texas.gov/ref/abouttx/secession/5march1861.html.

47. Quoted in Miller, *Lincoln*, 2:103.

48. Quoted in Miller, *Lincoln*, 2:103.

49. Quoted in Miller, *Lincoln*, 2:115.

50. Quoted in Miller, *Lincoln*, 2:120.

51. *Vandalia Illinois State Register*, Jan. 23 or 24 (dating inconsistent this issue), 1837; Miller, *Lincoln*, 2:120–121.

52. Miller, *Lincoln*, 2:121.

53. Miller, *Lincoln*, 2:561, n. 203.

54. Miller, *Lincoln*, 2:122–123.

55. *Congressional Globe*, 23:1, Jan. 27, 1834, pp. 129–130.

56. *Congressional Globe*, 24:1, March 31, 1836, p. 308.

57. *Congressional Globe*, 24:1, April 22, 1836, p. 335.

58. *Congressional Globe*, 24:1, June 28, 1836, p. 591.

59. Quoted in Miller, *Lincoln*, 4:78.

60. Quoted in Miller, *Lincoln*, 4:78.

61. Miller, *Lincoln*, 4:79, 85.

62. Quoted in Squire, *Right*, 94.

63. *Congressional Globe*, 33:1, March 7, 1854, p. 550.

64. Smith, *Congressional Globe*, 25:2, p. 223.

65. *Congressional Globe*, 25:3, Feb. 22, 1839, p. 198.

66. Guild, *Old*, 146–147, 150.

67. *Congressional Globe*, 23:2, March 3, 1835, p. 324.

68. *Congressional Globe*, 25:2, July 2, 1838, p. 466.

69. *Congressional Globe*, 26:2, Jan. 28, Feb. 5, 1841.

Notes—Part One

70. *Congressional Globe*, 27:1, June 22, 1841.
71. *Congressional Globe*, 26:2, Feb. 18, 20, 1841, pp. 186, 197–198.
72. *Congressional Globe*, 25:3, Feb. 22, 1839, p. 198.
73. Osgood, *Congressional Globe*, 23:1, May 5, 1834, p. 364.
74. *Congressional Globe*, 26:2, Jan. 14, 1841.
75. Grundy, *Congressional Globe*, 25:2, Feb. 6, 1838.
76. *Congressional Globe*, 25:2, July 2, 1838, p. 467.
77. *Congressional Globe*, 25:2, July 2, 1838, p. 467.
78. *Congressional Globe*, 23:2, March 3, 1835, p. 324.
79. *Congressional Globe*, 25:3, Jan. 9, 1839, p. 102. See also *Congressional Globe*, 31:1, Jan. 8, 1850, p. 122.
80. *Congressional Globe*, 27:2, April 29, 1842, p. 454.
81. *Congressional Globe*, 25:3, Jan. 9, 1839, p. 102.
82. *Congressional Globe*, 31:1, Jan. 8, 1850.
83. *Congressional Globe*, 31:1, Jan. 28, 1850, p. 230.
84. Douglas, Dec. 23, 1851, quoted in Flint and Douglas, *Life*, 61–62.
85. *Congressional Globe*, 31:1, March 25, 1850, p. 590.
86. *Congressional Globe*, 33:1, April 11, 1854, p. 885.
87. *Congressional Globe*, 31:1, Jan. 8, 1850, pp. 97–98.
88. *Congressional Globe*, 26:1, March 24, 1840, p. 257.
89. *Congressional Globe*, 25:2, July 2, 1838, p. 467.
90. *Congressional Globe*, 31:1, July 3, 1854.
91. *Congressional Globe*, 31:1, Jan. 8, 10, 1850, p. 119.
92. *Congressional Globe*, 31:1, Jan. 8, 1850, p. 120, March 8, p. 493.
93. *Congressional Globe*, 33:1, May 25, 1854, p. 1321.
94. *Congressional Globe*, 33:1, March 20, 1854, p. 678.
95. *Congressional Globe*, 35:1, Feb. 23, 1858, p. 804.
96. *Congressional Globe*, 35:1, Feb. 23, 1858, p. 809.
97. *Congressional Globe*, 33:1, Feb. 17, 1854, p. 442.
98. *Congressional Globe*, 33:1, March 30, 1854, p. 803.
99. *Congressional Globe*, 33:1, March 7, 1854, p. 550.
100. Lincoln, Sept. 12, 1854.
101. *Congressional Globe*, 24:1, March 31, 1836.
102. *Congressional Globe*, 27:2, April 14, 1842, p. 422.
103. *Congressional Globe*, 31:1, March 22, 1850, p. 584.
104. Walker, *Congressional Globe*, 25:2, Feb. 25, 1838.
105. *Congressional Globe*, 27:2, April 29, 1842, p. 454.
106. *Congressional Globe*, 33:1, Dec. 21, 1853, p. 73 (maritime). See also maritime instructions by Maryland legislature, *Congressional Globe*, April 9, 1850.
107. *Congressional Globe*, 26:1, Feb. 17, 1840, p. 201.
108. *Congressional Globe*, 31:1, April 9, 1850, p. 670.
109. *Congressional Globe*, 1850, *passim*.
110. *Congressional Globe*, 25:2, Feb. 5, 1838.
111. *Congressional Globe*, 27:2, April 20, 1842, p. 432.
112. *Congressional Globe*, 25:3, Jan. 23, 1839, p. 133.
113. *Congressional Globe*, 31:1, April 12, 1850, p. 720.
114. *Congressional Globe*, 31:1, April 4, 1850, p. 637.
115. *Congressional Globe*, 31:1, April 15, 1850, p. 730.
116. *Congressional Globe*, 25:2, May 24, 1838, p. 409.
117. *Congressional Globe*, 31:1, p. 231.

118. *Congressional Globe*, 31:1, Feb. 6, 1850, p. 299.
119. *Congressional Globe*, 33:1, April 26, 1854, p. 1001.
120. *Congressional Globe*, 26:2, Feb. 1, 1841, p. 135.
121. *Congressional Globe*, 26:2, Jan. 14, 1841, p. 99.
122. *Congressional Globe*, 27:2, April 29, 1842, p. 454.
123. *Congressional Record*, May 8, 1882, p. 3688.
124. Congressional Record, 1911, p. 4301.

Part Two

1. John M. Scott, quoted in Tarbell, *Life*, 1:193–194.
2. *Congressional Record*, 52:1, March 7, 1892, pp. 1807–1808.
3. Andrew A. Zellers-Frederick, "The Impeachment of Senator William Blount—the First in American History," quoted in *Journal of the American Revolution*, February 16, 2021.
4. Abigail Adams to Mary Smith Cranch, July 6, 1797.
5. *Congressional Globe*, 37:2, Jan. 30.
6. *Congressional Globe*, 37:2, June 21, 1862, p. 2850.
7. James F. Simmons, Report of Committee, USS, July 14, 1862, U.S. Congressional Serial Set, v. 3069, 37:2, pp. 754–756.
8. *Journal* of the Senate of the United States of America, 37:2, July 2, 1862.
9. Quoted in Crippen, *Simon*, 61.
10. James Polk quoted in Crippen, *Simon*, 82.
11. McClure, quoted in Crippen, *Simon*, 69.
12. Tarbell, *Life*, 2:134.
13. Tarbell, *Life*, 2:135.
14. Caldwell, "Pomeroy's," 463.
15. Quoted in Caldwell, "Pomeroy's," 463.
16. Caldwell, "Pomeroy's," 464.
17. Caldwell, "Pomeroy's," 465.
18. Quoted in Caldwell, "Pomeroy's."
19. Cutler 1873.
20. "The Election Case of John J. Ingalls of Kansas (1880)," in Anne M. Butler and Wendy Wolff, *United States Senate Election, Expulsion, and Censure Cases, 1793–1990*, S. Doc. 103–33 (Washington, D.C.: Government Printing Office, 1995). See also https://www.senate.gov/about/origins-foundations/electing-appointing-senators/contested-senate-elections/072John_Ingalls.htm.
21. U.S. Senate Committee on Privileges and Elections, Feb. 17, 1880, 1, 3–4, 24–26, 29, 41, 35, 84, 91.
22. Report of the Select Committee to Investigate Charges of Bribery in Connection with the Election of Hon. Henry B. Payne, as United States Senator, by the Sixty-Sixth General Assembly of Ohio, to the House of Representatives of the Sixty-Seventh General Assembly, Columbus, Ohio, 1886.
23. Burke, "Henry," 30.
24. *U.S. v. Dietrich*, 126 F. 664 (1904).
25. Quoted in Bourne, *Congressional Record*, 61:2, May 5, 1910, p. 5826.
26. Quoted in Wikipedia entry for William A. Clark.
27. *Records and Briefs of the United States Supreme Court*, v. 202, p. 164.
28. *Records and Briefs of the United States Supreme Court*, v. 202, p. 131.
29. *Records and Briefs of the United States Supreme Court*, v. 202, pp. 131, 149; *Burton* v. *United States*, 196 U.S. 283 (1905); *Burton* v. *United States*, 202 U.S. 344 (1906).
30. Puter and Stevens, *Looters*, 63.
31. *Martinsburg [WV] Herald*, Jan. 28, 1911; U.S. Senate, "Compilation of Senate Election Cases from 1789 to 1913," 62:3, Doc. 1036, serial set 5800 to 6599.
32. Steffens, "Shame," Oct. 1903.
33. Croly, *Marcus*, 259.
34. U.S. Senate, 55:3, Report 1859, Feb. 28, 1899; Richard Pettigrew, *Congressional Record*, June 5, 1900.

Notes—Part Three

35. Butler and Wolff, *United States Senate Election, Expulsion, and Censure Cases*; LaForte, "Gilded Age Senator," *Kansas History*; Cutler, *History of the State of Kansas*.
36. Puter and Stevens, *Looters*, 12–13.
37. Quoted in Schiller and Stewart III, *Electing*, 59.

Part Three

1. Peoria speech, Oct. 16, 1854.
2. June 17, 1854.
3. *Illinois Daily Journal*, May 24, 1854.
4. *Alton Daily Courier*, extra ed., Oct. 30, 1854.
5. Shields to Charles Lanphier, Oct. 25, 1854, Patton, *Glory*, v. 3.
6. W. [Horace White?], *Daily Chicago Journal*, Oct. 5, 1854.
7. A. Jones to Lincoln, Nov. 22, 1854.
8. E. Powell to Lincoln, Nov. 16, 1854.
9. Washburne to Lincoln, Dec. 26, 1854.
10. Nicolay and Hay, *Abraham*, 1:385.
11. Ramsey to Lincoln, Dec. 23, 1854.
12. A. Jonas to Lincoln, Sept. 16, 1854.
13. W. Randolph to Lincoln, Sept. 29, 1854.
14. George Gage to Lincoln, Oct. 4, 1854.
15. Horace White to Lincoln, Oct. 25, 1854.
16. T. Dickey to Lincoln, Nov. 19, 1854.
17. A. Jonas to Lincoln, Dec. 2, 1854.
18. Lincoln to J. Scammon, Nov. 10; to C. Hoyt, Nov. 10; to J. Harding, Nov. 11; to T. Henderson, Nov. 27; to H. LeMaster, Nov. 29; to J. Gillespie, Dec. 1; to E. Washburne, Dec. 14; to T. Henderson, Dec. 15, 1854.
19. W. Fithian, Nov. 20, 1854.
20. T. Henderson to Lincoln, Dec. 11, 1854.
21. H. Johns to Lincoln, Nov. 15, 1854.
22. T. Marshall to Lincoln, Dec. 8, 1854.
23. R. Servant to Lincoln, Dec. 2, 1854.
24. W. Henderson to Lincoln, Dec. 11, 1854.
25. L. Swett to Lincoln, Dec. 22, 1854.
26. T. Turner to Lincoln, Dec. 10, 1854.
27. Washburne to Lincoln, Nov. 14, 1854.
28. Davis to Lincoln, Dec. 26, 1854.
29. *Congressional Globe*, 31:1, April 5, 1850, pp. 649–560.
30. Trumbull to John Palmer, Nov. 23, 1854 ("Collection," 20–23).
31. Sheahan to Lanphier, Jan. 17, 1855 (Patton, *Glory*, v. 3).
32. Quoted in Donald, *Lincoln's*, 78.
33. Quoted in Fischer, "Samuel," 11.
34. Miller, *Lincoln*, 4:193, 272. See also *Chicago Press and Tribune*, Oct. 25, 1858, and Koerner, *Memoirs*, 2:37.
35. Lincoln to B. Lundy, Aug. 5, 1857.
36. Quoted in Fehrenbacher, *Prelude*, 49. See also clipping in *Daily Illinois State Register*, Nov. 13, 1858.
37. Charleston debate, Sept. 18, 1858.
38. M. Inman to Lincoln, Nov. 9, 1858.
39. Lincoln to M. Inman, Nov. 20, 1858.
40. Miller, *Lincoln*, 4:221.
41. Miller, *Lincoln*, 4:269–270.
42. *Rock Island Morning Argus*, June 3, 1857.
43. *Congressional Record*, March 4, 1911, p. 4296.
44. *Congressional Record*, March 4, 1911, p. 4295.
45. *Congressional Record*, March 4, 1911, pp. 4296 ff.
46. *Congressional Record*, March 4, 1911, p. 4300.
47. *The Shame of the City*, chapter "Tweed Days in St. Louis."

Bibliography

Adams, John. Papers.

Annals of Congress. Compiled by Joseph Gales and William Seaton.

Bernstein, Peter L. *Wedding of the Waters: The Erie Canal and the Making of a Great Nation.* New York: W.W. Norton, 2005.

Brugh, James. *Political Disquisitions: Or, an inquiry Into Public Errors.* London: Bell & Woodhouse, 1774.

Burke, Dewayne. "Henry B. Payne: His Congressional Career" (M.A. thesis). The Ohio State University, 1938.

Butler, Anne M., and Wendy Wolff. *United States Senate Election, Expulsion, and Censure Cases, 1793–1990.* S. Doc. 103-33. Washington, D.C.: Government Printing Office, 1995.

Caldwell, Martha B. "Pomeroy's 'Ross Letter': Genuine or Forgery?" *Kansas Historical Quarterly* 13 (Aug. 1944), 463–472.

Congressional Quarterly.

Crippen, Lee Forbes. *Simon Cameron, Ante-bellum Years.* Oxford: Mississippi Valley Press, 1942.

Croly, Herbert David. *Marcus Alonzo Hanna, His Life and Work.* New York: Macmillan, 1912.

Cutler, William G. *History of the State of Kansas,* "Legislative and Political Annals," Part 16. Chicago: A.T. Andreas, 1883.

Donald, David Herbert. *Lincoln's Herndon.* New York: Da Capo Press, 1989. Reprint of New York: Alfred A. Knopf, 1948.

Eaton, Clement. "Southern Senators and the Right of Instruction, 1789–1860." *Journal of Southern History*18, no. 3 (Aug. 1952), 303–319.

Eliott's *Debates* (referring to early debates of U.S. Congress).

Fehrenbacher, Don E. *Prelude to Greatness.* Stanford: Stanford University Press, 1962

Fischer, LeRoy H. "Samuel C. Parks Reminiscences of Abraham Lincoln." *Lincoln Herald* 68 (1966), 11–19.

Flint, Henry Martyn, and Stephen Arnold Douglas. *Life of Stephen A. Douglas: With His Most Important Speeches and Reports.* New York: Derby & Jackson, 1860.

Guild, Joseph C. *Old Times in Tennessee with Historical, Personal, and Political Scraps and Sketches.* Nashville: Tavel, Eastman & Howell, 1878.

"Illinois' Senatorial Scandal." *The Voter* XII (May 1911) and XIII (March 1912).

Kiger, Patrick J. "Musketgate." Retrieved from https://www.historynet.com/musketgate/. This article appears in the Spring 2018 issue (30, no. 3) of *MHQ—The Quarterly Journal of Military History* with the headline "Musketgate."

Koerner, Gustave. *Memoirs of Gustave*

Bibliography

Koerner, 1809–1896. 2 vols. Thomas J. McCormack, ed. Cedar Rapids: Torch Press, 1909.

LaForte, Robert S. "Gilded Age Senator." *Kansas History* 21:4 (Winter 1998–1999).

Lowry, Sharon K. "Portrait of an Age: The Political Career of Stephen W. Dorsey, 1868–1889." Dissertation. North Texas State University, 1980.

Massaro, John. *No Guarantee of a Gun: How and Why the Second Amendment Means Exactly What It Says*. Bloomington: AuthorHouse, 2008.

Miller, Richard Lawrence. *Lincoln and His World*. Vol. 2. Mechanicsburg, PA: Stackpole Books, 2006. Vol. 4. Jefferson, NC: McFarland, 2010.

Nicolay, John G., and John Hay. *Abraham Lincoln: A History*. New York: The Century Co., 1890.

Patton, Charles C. *Glory to God and the Sucker Democracy: A Manuscript Collection of the Letters of Charles H. Lanphier*. Springfield, IL: By the Author, 1973.

Petyt, William. *The Ancient Right of the Commons of England Asserted, or, a Discourse Proving by Records and the Best Historians that the Commons of England were Ever an Essential Part of Parliament*.

Puter, S.A.D., and Horace Stevens. *Looters of the Public Domain*. Portland, OR: The Portland Printing House, 1908.

Report of the Majority. Select Committee to Investigate Charges of Bribery in Connection with the Election of Hon. Henry B. Payne as United States Senator, by the Sixty-Sixth General Assembly of Ohio, to the House of Representatives of the Sixty-Seventh General Assembly.

Report of the Select Committee to Investigate Charges of Bribery in Connection With the Election of Hon. Henry B. Payne, as United States Senator, by the Sixty-Sixth General Assembly of Ohio, to the House of Representatives of the Sixty-Seventh General Assembly. Columbus, OH, 1886.

Roane, A. "Right of Instruction." *Southern Literary Messenger* 2 (Oct. 1836), 684–692.

  This source, while useful, is troublesome. The author's name appears to be a pen name, which admittedly can be dismissed as merely a custom of the era. More disturbing is my frequent inability to verify his sources. For instance, I am unable to find a copy of the 1776 Virginia Bill of Rights from which he claims to quote on p. 688 in the lower part of the left column. As indicated by my reference notes, I find Roane's article to be useful, but I suggest scrutiny before accepting his statements.

Schiller, Wendy J., and Charles Stewart III. *Electing the Senate: Indirect Democracy before the Seventeenth Amendment*. Princeton: Princeton University Press, 2015.

Scott, Nancy N. *A Memoir of Hugh Lawson White*. New York: J.B. Lippincott, 1856.

Squire, Peverill. *The Right of Instruction and Representation in American Legislatures, 1778 to 1900*. Ann Arbor: University of Michigan Press, 2021.

Steffens, Lincoln. "The Shame of the Cities." *McClure's Magazine*, Oct. 1903.

Taft, George S., George P. Furber, and George M. Buck. *Compilation of Senate Election Cases From 1789 to 1885*. Washington, D.C.: Government Printing Office, 1903. U.S. Senate Doc. 11. 58 Congress, Special Session.

Bibliography

Tarbell, Ida M. *The Life of Abraham Lincoln*. New York: Macmillan, 1928.

Topeka Daily Capital, Topeka, 1879.

U.S. Congressional Serial Set Reports of Committees of the U.S. Senate 46:1 & 2, 1879. Washington, D.C.: GPO Hearings and Reports 277, U.S. Senate Committee on Privileges and Elections, Feb 17, 1880. "Investigation of Charges in Relation to the Election of John J. Ingalls."

    See also https://www.senate.gov/about/origins-foundations/electing-appointing-senators/contested-senate-elections/pdf/72_Feb_17_1880_Ingalls.pdf.

    See also William C. Webb. *The Ingalls Case: A Review of the Investigations of John J. Ingalls, United States Senator from Kansas Upon Charges of Bribing and Corrupting Members of the Kansas Legislature to Secure His Re-election.*

United States v. Dietrich, United States Circuit Court for the District of Nebraska 126 F. 664 (Jan. 4, 1904).

U.S. Senate. "Compilation of Senate Election Cases from 1789 to 1913." 62:3, Doc. 1036, pp. 637–41, serial set 5800 to 6599.

U.S. Senate, 55:3, Report 1859, Feb. 28, 1899.

U.S. Senate. James F. Simmons, Report of Committee, USS, July 14, 1862, U.S. Congressional Serial Set, v. 3069, 37:2, pp. 754–756.

U.S. Supreme Court. *Records and Briefs*, v. 202, Oct. term, 1905, no. 539.

Index

Numbers in ***bold italics*** indicate pages with illustrations

Adams, Abigail 47–48, ***47***
Adams, John 6, 11
Amendment Seventeen 43
Ames, Fisher 14
arms contracts 51, ***52***, 54, 55
Articles of Confederation 16
Atchison, David 35

Bank of the U.S. (First) 27–28
Bank of the U.S. (Second) 27–32
banking policy 25
Bell, Samuel 31
Benton, Thomas Hart ***29***, 35
Blount, William 46–49, ***49***
Brent, Richard 28
Brugh, James 12–13
Bright, Jesse 49–51, ***49***
Britain 12–13
Buchanan, James 14, ***14***
Burton, Joseph ***76***, 76–77

Caldwell, Alexander 85–86
Cameron, Simon 36, 55–57, ***56***
Chilton, William 80
civil liberties 19–22, 33
Clark, William 73–76, ***74, 75***
Clay, Henry 28, 40
Clayton, John 29, 33
Clymer, George 20
colonial 6
confederate states insurrection 21
Conkling, Roscoe 87–88
Constitution, U.S. 16–17
constitutions, state and Territorial: Arkansas 18; Florida 18; Georgia 16; Illinois 21–22; Kansas 18; Maine 18; Maryland 16; Massachusetts 19; Michigan 18; New York 16, 18; North Carolina 19; Ohio 19; Pennsylvania 16; Rhode Island 18; Vermont 18, 19
Crockett, John 9, ***9***

Dietrich, Charles 70–71
Dorsey, Stephen ***62, 63***, 62–66
Douglas, Stephen 23–24, ***24***, 26, 34, 37–38, 94–95, 97, 100–101

electors 43
Ewing, Thomas 25

Fessenden, William 30
foreign customs 11–12
Foster, Epheraim 32
Franklin, Benjamin 11
Frelinghuysen, Theodore 32–33

Gerry, Elbridge 21
gerrymandering 103–104
Giles William Branch 28
Graham, William A. 15
Grundy, Felix 32
Guild, Joseph 31–32

Hamilton, Alexander 17–18
Hamlin, Hannibal 37
Hanna, Marcus ***83, 84***, 85
Hardin, John 22, ***23***
Hill, Isaac 25, 31
Howe, Timothy 50
Hubbard, Henry 25

Independent Treasury Act 28, 29
Ingalls, John 59–62, ***60***

121

Index

Jackson, Andrew 28; censure 28–29, *29*
Jefferson, Thomas 17

King, Rufus 17
King, William R. 31

Leigh, Benjamin Watkins 28
Lincoln, Abraham 22; 1854 U.S. Senate campaign 37, 91; 1855 U.S. Senate campaign 26, 101; 1858 U.S. Senate campaign 102–103; 1859 U.S. Senate campaign 101
local customs 21–24
Lorimer, William *80*, 80–83
Lytle, Robert 24–25

MacDonald, Moses 35
Mangum, Willie 33
Matthews, Stanley 86–87
McClernand, John 23, 92
McKean, Samuel 29, 39
Miller, Jacob 35
Mitchell, John Hipple *78*, 78–79
Moore, Gabriel 31
Morris, Thomas 25

Niles, John 7, 30

Osgood Gayton 30
Owen, Robert 42, 105–106

Page, Thomas 21
Payne, Henry *66*, *67*, *68*, *69*, 66–70
Pickens, Francis 9, *10*
Platt, Thomas 86–87
Pomeroy, Samuel 57–59, *58*
Prentiss, Samuel 33
Progressives 89–90, 103, 105–108

Quay, Matthew 90

railroads 104
Rialto Grain and Securities Company 76–77

Richardson, William 93
Rives, William Cabell 29–30
Robinson, John 30

Schubarth, Casper 52–53
Senate corruption 45, 87–88, *88*, 105, 107–108
Senate election deadlock 89
Senate legislative agenda 89
Seward, William 36
Sherman, John 20–21
Shields, James 92, 95, 99–101
Simmons, James *51*, *52*, 51–55
slavery 33–36, *56*, 57
Smith, Perry 7, 30
Smith, Thomas 16
Stamp Act protests 7, 8
Stanton, Edwin 51, 54
Stephenson, Isaac 71–73
Strange, Robert 15
Sturgeon, Daniel 41
Subtreasury Act *see* Independent Treasury Act

Tallmadge, Nathanial 29
Trumbull, Lyman 26, *27*, 93, 100–101
Tucker, Thomas Tudor 20
Turpie, David 85
Tyler, John 30

Van Buren, Martin 31

Walker, Robert 38
Washington, George 48
Watson, Clarence 79, *79*
White, Hugh 32
Williams, Archie 93
Williams, Reuel 30
Wilmot, David 51
Wright, Silas 26, 29

Yates, Richard 93
Young, Richard 31, 38

www.ingramcontent.com/pod-product-compliance
Ingram Content Group UK Ltd.
Pitfield, Milton Keynes, MK11 3LW, UK
UKHW042017140426
5217IPUK00015B/1223